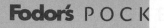

Fodor's P O C K

D0790053

dublin

Excerpted from *Fodor's Ireland 2001*

fodor's travel publications

new york · toronto · london · sydney · auckland

www.fodors.com

contents

maps

ON THE ROAD WITH FODOR'S

EVERY TRIP IS A SIGNIFICANT TRIP. Acutely aware of that fact, we've pulled out all stops in preparing *Fodor's Pocket Dublin*. To guide you in putting together your Dublin experience, we've created multiday itineraries and regional tours. And to direct you to the places that are truly worth your time and money, we've rallied the team of endearingly picky know-it-alls we're pleased to call our writers. Having seen all corners of Dublin, they're real experts. If you knew them, you'd poll them for tips yourself.

ANTO HOWARD—who worked on the Here and There, Shopping, Outdoor Activities and Sports, Nightlife and the Arts, Where to Stay and Practical Information chapters—is a Northside Dublin native who studied at Trinity College before acquiring his U.S. green card. He moved to New York, where he is currently a travel writer, editor, and playwright. He has written numerous articles on Ireland, Central America, Russia, and the United States.

ORNA MULCAHY, who revised the Eating Out chapter, is a journalist and restaurant critic with the *Irish Times* newspaper in Dublin.

Don't Forget to Write

Keeping a travel guide fresh and up-to-date is a big job. So we love your feedback—positive and negative—and follow up on all suggestions. Contact the Pocket Dublin editor at editorsfodors.com or c/o Fodor's, 280 Park Avenue, New York, New York 10017. And have a wonderful trip!

Karen Cure

Karen Cure

Editorial Director

Distance Conversion Chart

Kilometers/Miles

To change kilometers (km) to miles (mi), multiply km by .621.
To change mi to km, multiply mi by 1.61.

km to mi	mi to km
1 = .62	1 = 1.6
2 = 1.2	2 = 3.2
3 = 1.9	3 = 4.8
4 = 2.5	4 = 6.4
5 = 3.1	5 = 8.1
6 = 3.7	6 = 9.7
7 = 4.3	7 = 11.3
8 = 5.0	8 = 12.9

Meters/Feet

To change meters (m) to feet (ft), multiply m by 3.28.
To change ft to m, multiply ft by .305.

m to ft	ft to m
1 = 3.3	1 = .30
2 = 6.6	2 = .61
3 = 9.8	3 = .92
4 = 13.1	4 = 1.2
5 = 16.4	5 = 1.5
6 = 19.7	6 = 1.8
7 = 23.0	7 = 2.1
8 = 26.2	8 = 2.4

ATLANTIC OCEAN

Tory Island

NORTHERN IRELAND
SCOTLAND

WALES   ENGLAND

Aran Island   Lette
Gweebarra
Bay   DO
Donegal
Town

Donegal   Ballyshannon
Bay

Killala   Sligo Bay
Bay   LEI
Ballina   Sligo Town
Lough   SLIGO
Conn
MAYO
Achill
Island   Castlebar
Clare Island   Clew Bay   ROSCOMMON
Inishturk   Knock
Inishbofin   Lough
Mask
CONNAUGHT
Lough
Corrib   Athlo
GALWAY   Galway   Ballinasloe
City   REPUB
Galway Bay
Aran
Islands   CLARE   Nenagh
Ennis   Limerick
City
Kilrush
LIMERICK   T
Mouth of   Listowel   Newcastle
the Shannon   West   C
Tralee   MUNSTER
Dingle Peninsula
Mallow
Blasket   Dingle Bay   Killarney   Fer
Islands   KERRY   CORK   Cork
Iveragh   City
Peninsula   Cob
Skellig   Bandon   Kinsale
Rocks   Kenmare Bay   Clonakilty
Bantry Bay   Skibbereen
Mizen Head

dublin

introducing dublin

THE ONLY ADEQUATE COMPARISON to the astonishing change that
has swept through Dublin in the last decade and continues
unabated today may be to the transformations underway in the
major cities of Central Europe—particularly Berlin, Prague, and
Budapest—in the wake of the revolutions of 1989. Geographically
the westernmost of European countries, Ireland underwent no
such profound historic, ideological upheaval as the revolutions
that sent its relatives on the eastern fringe of Europe, for decades
firmly locked behind the Iron Curtain, careening into the present.
And yet, the scope of what is happening in Ireland's capital
suggests that something almost as momentous has happened
here—even if it's not possible to pinpoint the precise moment,
as we can down to the day, that set in motion the rebirth of
Central Europe. Even if the pace of change that has gripped
Dublin in the 1990s has not been as politically profound as that
underway at the other end of Europe, it has been no less furious.

How dramatic are the changes taking place? On a wintry November
day in the fall of 1996, a visitor to Dublin counted 18 construction
cranes from the sixth-story roof of his center-city hotel—18
massive cranes towering over the Dublin skyline, poised over
shiny new hotels and old Georgian houses, each signifying
commitments of large sums of money and a deep faith in the city's
future. Is it an accident that in several scenes in the 1991 film *The
Commitments* you can glimpse one of these cranes quietly whispering
off in the distance—a portent of things to come? The cranes, of
course, are just the most outsized signs of Dublin's vitality. For

every crane there are hundreds of stories of transformation in this city, both big and tall and small and quiet.

But first, to Dublin's past. Its origins as a village date back some 1,500 years, when it was little more than a crossroads—albeit a critical one—of four of the main thoroughfares that traversed the country. It has two names dating back this far: Baile Atha Cliath (City of the Hurdles), bestowed by Celtic traders in the 2nd century AD and which you can still see on buses and billboards throughout the city, and Dubhlinn or "dark pool," which is believed to have been where Dublin Castle now stands. Today, the area where the city's first inhabitants built their dwellings is known as the Liberties; sections of the first town walls, dating back nearly 1,000 years, can still be seen off Thomas Street, west of Christ Church Cathedral.

In 837, Norsemen from Scandinavia carried out the first outside attack on Dublin, arriving in a fleet of 60 longboats. Four years later, the Vikings built their first port here and used it for raiding large tracts of the countryside. Despite Irish resistance against Viking rule, the Norsemen made Dublin one of the principal centers of their empire, which stretched from Russia to Ireland to Iceland. The power of the Scandinavians was finally broken by the Irish at the Battle of Clontarf in 1014, which took place north of Dublin. Native rule, however, was short-lived. The Anglo-Normans landed in County Wexford, in southeast Ireland, in 1169; a mere two years later, King Henry II of England finally subdued some of the Irish chieftains and granted Dublin its first charter.

Through the Middle Ages, the city developed as a trading center, though fraught with political difficulties. The last remaining relic of medieval trade in Ireland can be seen nearly opposite Christ Church Cathedral, in Tailor's Hall. In 1651, English soldier Oliver Cromwell occupied and ransacked Dublin, which at the time was still little more than a large village with 15,000 inhabitants. Not until the 18th century did Dublin reach a period of glory, when a golden age of enlightened patronage by wealthy members of the nobility turned the city into one of Europe's most prepossessing cities. New streets and squares, such as Merrion and Fitzwilliam Squares, were constructed with a classical dignity and elegance. Handel, the German-born English composer, wrote much of his great oratorio, the *Messiah*, in Dublin, where it was first performed in 1742. Many other crafts, such as bookbinding and solver making, flourished to cater to the needs of the often-titled and usually wealthy members of society. Ireland was granted a certain measure of political autonomy by the British, and in the new government buildings (now the Bank of Ireland) in College Green, opposite Trinity College, the independent parliament met for the first time in 1783. Throughout this period, until the early 19th century, social and economic power rested exclusively in Protestant hands.

The glory of this era was short-lived; in 1800, the Act of Union brought Ireland and Britain together in a common United Kingdom, and the seat of political power and patronage moved form Dublin to London. Dublin quickly lost its cultural and social sparkle, as many members of the nobility moved to London. The 19th century proved to be a time of political turmoil and agitation, although Daniel O'Connell, a lord mayor of Dublin, won early success with the introduction of Catholic emancipation in 1829. During the late 1840s, Dublin escaped the worst effects of the famine, caused by potato disease, that blighted much of southern and western Ireland. New industries, such as mineral-water manufacturing, were established, and with an emerging Victorian middle class introducing an element of genteel snobbery to the city, Dublin began its rapid outward expansion. Until the mid-19th century, Dublin extended little beyond St. Stephen's green, but with the sudden demand for additional housing by the newly wealthy, many new suburbs were established, such as Ballsbridge, Rathgar, and Rathmimes on the southside, and Clontarf and Drumcondra on the northside.

In the first decade of this century, Dublin entered a period of cultural ferment—an era that had its political apotheosis in the Easter Uprising of 1916, which lasted a week, damaging many buildings in and around O'Connell Street on the northside of the city center. In 1919, the war aimed at winning independence from Britain began in County Tipperary and lasted for three years. Dublin was comparatively unscathed during this period, but during the Civil War, which followed the setting up of the Irish Free State in December 1921, more harm came to a number of the city's historic buildings, including the Four Courts and the Custom House, which both burned down. The capital had to be rebuilt during the 1920s. After the Civil War was over, Dublin entered a new era of political and cultural conservatism, which continued until the late 1950s. In the 1960s, an era of economic optimism pervaded the city, but much of this enthusiasm waned again during the recessionary years of the 1970s.

If there was a major turning point in Dublin's fortunes in the last 25 years, it was in the 1980s, when Irish musicians stormed the American and British barricades of rock and roll. Bob Geldof and the Boomtown Rats ("I Don't Like Mondays") and Chris de Burgh were among the most prominent Irish musicians who found audiences well beyond Irish shores, but it was U2, which ascended the farthest heights of rock-and-roll stardom, that forever changed the place of Irish musicians in international popular culture. Sinéad O'Connor and The Cranberries have since followed, and it's certain that more are on the way.

If the 1980s saw the ascent of Irish rock stars, the 1990s truly were the boom years—a decade of broadly improved economic fortunes, major capital investment, declining unemployment, and reversing patterns of immigration—all set in motion to a great extent by Ireland's participation in the European Union, or EU. When Ireland approved the EU in 1992, it was one of the poorest European nations; it qualified for EU grants of all kinds. Money has, quite simply, poured into Ireland—nowhere more so than in Dublin. The International Financial Services Centre, gleaming behind the two-centuries-old Custom House, is just one of the most overt signs of the success the city has had in attracting leading multinational corporations into the city, particularly in telecommunications, software, and service industries. But Dublin's swift transformation is probably a result not only of macroeconomic changes but of more grassroots changes, as well. To discover just how generous and widespread the EU grant-giving has been here, ask any random Dubliners whether they know any individual who has received a grant, and see what they say.

Today roughly half of the Irish Republic's population of 3.6 million people live in Dublin and its suburbs. It is a young city—astonishingly so. Students from all over Ireland attend Trinity College and the city's dozen other universities. On weekends, their counterparts from Paris, London, and Rome fly in, swelling the city's youthful contingent. After graduating from university, more and more young Irish men and women are sticking around rather than emigrating to New York or London, filling the raft of new jobs, and contributing to the hubbub that's evident everywhere in the city. The city is also increasingly as heterogeneous as it is young, for as multinational corporations have set up shop in Dublin, a large number of Middle Easterners and many American, Dutch, German, and Japanese immigrants have settled here. Today, more and more Americans of Irish descent are obtaining citizenship and returning to the capital of the country their ancestors left 150 years ago during the Great Famine.

James Joyce immortalized Dublin in his short stories and his modernist masterpiece, *Ulysses*, filling his works with the people he knew, with their own words and the cadence of their Dublin patois. He was also one of Dublin's—and Ireland's—most famous exiles. In 1902, at the age of 20, he left Dublin and thereafter returned only for brief visits. (Samuel Beckett, his assistant and friend, followed him into exile.) Walking around the buzzing boomtown of Dublin today, you have to ask yourself, would Joyce have forsaken "our dear, dirty Dublin," as he so famously called his hometown, were he alive today? What would he have made of this genteel city, a place that seems astonished at its newfound fortunes?

In This Chapter

Updated by Anto Howard

here and there

"IN DUBLIN'S FAIR CITY, where the girls are so pretty" went the centuries-old ditty. Today, parts of the city—particularly the vast, uniform housing projects of the northern suburbs—may not be fair or pretty. But even if you're not conscious of it while you're in the city center, Dublin is in a beautiful setting: it loops around the edge of Dublin Bay and on a plain at the edge of the gorgeous, green Dublin and Wicklow mountains, rising softly just to the south. From the famous Four Courts building in the heart of town, the sight of the city, the bay, and the mountains will take your breath away. From the city's noted vantage points, such as the South Wall, which stretches far out into Dublin Bay, or from choice spots in the suburbs of south and north County Dublin, you can nearly get a full measure of the city. From north to south, Dublin stretches 16 km (10 mi). From its center, immediately adjacent to the port area and the River Liffey, the city spreads westward for an additional 10 km (6 mi); in total, it covers 28,000 acres. But its heart is far more compact than these numbers indicate. As in Paris, London, and Florence, and as in so many other cities throughout the world, a river runs right through Dublin. The River Liffey divides the capital into the "northside" and the "southside," as everyone calls the two principal center-city areas, and almost all the major sights in the area are well within less than an hour's walk of one another.

Coverage is organized into eight walks of the city center and the areas immediately surrounding it, and two excursions into County Dublin—the first to the southern suburbs, the latter to the northern. The first two walks—The Center City: Around Trinity College and The Georgian Heart of Dublin—cover many of the southside's major sites: Trinity College, St. Stephen's Green, Merrion Square, and Grafton Street. It makes sense to do these walks first, as they will quickly orient you to a good portion of the southside. The third walk—Temple Bar: Dublin's "Left Bank"—takes you through this revived neighborhood, which is the hottest, hippest zone in the capital. The fourth walk—Dublin West: From Dublin Castle to the Four Courts—picks up across the street from Temple Bar and gets you to the Guinness Brewery, the city's most popular attraction. The fifth walk—The Liberties—takes you on a brief stroll through working-class Dublin, a historic but often overlooked part of the city. A word about these five walks: although we've split the southside into five, you'll soon realize that the distance between the areas in all these walks is not very great. The sixth walk—North of the Liffey—moves to the northside of the city center and covers all the major cultural sites there, including the James Joyce Cultural Centre, Gate Theatre, Dublin Writers Museum, and Hugh Lane Municipal Gallery of Modern Art. It also includes the rapidly developing Smithfield district, which locals are already hailing the future "Temple Bar of the northside." The seventh walk—Along the Grand Canal—covers noteworthy sites along the canal, beginning in the northeast part of the city, and ending in the southwest. Phoenix Park and Environs, at the western fringe of the northside city center, is the main focus of the eighth Dublin walk.

Because of its compact size and traffic congestion (brought on in the last few years by an astronomical increase in the number of new vehicles), *pedestrian* traffic—especially on the city center's busiest streets during commute hours—is astonishing. Watch where you stop to consult your map or you're liable to be swept away by the ceaseless flow of the bustling crowds.

Numbers in the text correspond to numbers in the margin and on the Dublin City Center and Dublin West maps.

THE CENTER CITY: AROUND TRINITY COLLEGE

The River Liffey provides a useful aid to orientation, flowing as it does through the direct middle of Dublin. If you ask a native Dubliner for directions—from under an umbrella, as it will probably be raining in the approved Irish manner—he or she will most likely reply in terms of "up" or "down," up meaning away from the river, and down toward it. Until recently, Dublin's center of gravity was O'Connell Bridge, a diplomatic landmark in that it avoided locating the center to the north or south of the river, as strong local loyalties still prevailed among "northsiders" (who live to the north of the river) and "southsiders," and neither would ever accept that the city's center lay on the other's side of the river. But by the early 1990s, diplomacy had gone by the wayside. Now, Dublin's heart beats loudest southward across the Liffey, due, in part, to a large-scale refurbishment and pedestrianization of Grafton Street, which made this already upscale shopping address the street to shop, stop, and be seen. At the foot of Grafton Street is the city's most famous and recognizable landmark, Trinity College; at the top of it is Dublin's most popular strolling retreat, St. Stephen's Green, a 27-acre landscaped park replete with flowers, lakes, bridges, and—most of all—Dubliners enjoying a time-out.

A Good Walk

Start at **Trinity College** ①, exploring the quadrangle as you head to the Old Library to see the *Book of Kells*. If you want to see modern art, visit the collection housed in the Douglas Hyde Gallery, just inside the Nassau Street entrance to the college. If you're interested in the Georgian era, try to view the Provost's House and its salon, the grandest in Ireland. Trinity can easily eat up at least an hour or more, so when you come back out the front gate, you can either stop in at the **Bank of Ireland** ②, a neoclassic masterpiece that was once the seat of the Irish Parliament, or make an immediate left and head up **Grafton Street** ③, the pedestrian spine of the southside. The **Dublin Tourism** ④ office is just off Grafton Street, on the corner of Suffolk Street. If Grafton Street's shops whet your appetite for more browsing and shopping, turn right down Wicklow Street, then left up South William Street to **Powerscourt Townhouse Centre** ⑤, where a faux-Georgian atrium (very dubiously set within one of Dublin's greatest 18th-century mansions) houses high-priced shops and pleasant cafés.

The **Dublin Civic Museum** ⑥ is next door to Powerscourt, across the alley on its south flank. If you're doing well on time and want to explore the shopping streets farther east, jog via the alley one block east to Drury Street, from which you can access the Victorian **George's Street Arcade** ⑦. Whether or not you make this excursion, you should head back to Grafton Street, where **Bewley's Oriental Café** ⑧, a Dublin institution, is another good place for a break. Grafton Street ends at the northwest corner of **St. Stephen's Green** ⑨, Dublin's most popular public gardens; they absolutely require a stroll-through. **Newman House** ⑩ is on the south side of the green. Amble back across the green, exiting onto the northeast corner, at which sits the grand **Shelbourne Méridien Hotel** ⑪, a wonderful place for afternoon tea or a quick pint at one of its two pubs. The **Huguenot Cemetery** ⑫ is just down the street from the hotel, on the same side. If you want to see more art, make a detour to the **RHA Gallagher Gallery** ⑬.

TIMING

Dublin's city center is so compact you could race through this walk in an hour, but in order to gain full advantage of what is on offer, we recommend that you set aside at least half a day—if you can—to explore the treasures of Trinity College and amble up and around Grafton Street to Stephen's Green.

Sights to See

❷ BANK OF IRELAND. Across the street from the west facade of **Trinity College** (☞ *below*) stands one of Dublin's most striking buildings, now the Bank of Ireland but formerly the original home of the Irish Parliament. The building was begun in 1729 by Sir Edward Lovett Pearce, who designed the central section; three other architects would ultimately be involved in its construction. A pedimented portico fronted by six massive Corinthian columns dominates its grand facade, which follows the curve of Westmoreland Street as it meets College Green, once a Viking meeting place and burial ground. Two years after the Parliament was abolished in 1801 under the Act of Union, which brought Ireland under the direct rule of Britain, the building was bought for £40,000 by the Bank of Ireland. Inside, stucco rosettes adorn the coffered ceiling in the pastel-hue, colonnaded, clerestoried **main banking hall,** at one time the Court of Requests, where citizens' petitions were heard. Just down the hall is the original **House of Lords,** with tapestries depicting the Battle of the Boyne and the Siege of Derry, an oak-paneled nave, and a 1,233-piece Waterford glass chandelier; ask a guard to show you in. Visitors are welcome during normal banking hours; a brief guided tour is given every Tuesday at 10:30, 11:30, and 1:45 by the Dublin historian and author Éamonn Mac Thomáis. Accessed via Foster Place South, the small alley on the bank's east flank, the **Bank of Ireland Arts Center** frequently exhibits contemporary Irish art and has a permanent exhibition devoted to "The Story of Banking." 2 *College Green, tel.* 01/677–6801, 01/671–1488 *arts center. Mon.–Wed. and Fri.* 10–4, *Thurs.* 10–5; *Arts Center Tues.–Fri.* 10–4, *Sat.* 2–5, *Sun.* 10–1.

❽ BEWLEY'S ORIENTAL CAFÉ. The granddaddies of the capital's cafés, Bewley's has been serving coffee and buns to Dubliners since it was founded by Quakers in 1842 and now has four locations. Bewley's trademark stained-glass windows were designed by Harry Clarke (1889–1931), Ireland's most distinguished early 20th-century artist in this medium. They all make fine places in which to observe Dubliners of all ages and occupations; the aroma of coffee is irresistible, and the cafés' dark interiors—with marble-top tables, bentwood chairs, and mahogany trim—evoke a more leisurely Dublin. The food is overpriced and not particularly good, but people-watching here over a cup of coffee or tea is a quintessential Dublin experience. If you're interested in a more modern cup of coffee, check out the Metro Café, nearby at 43 South

dublin city center

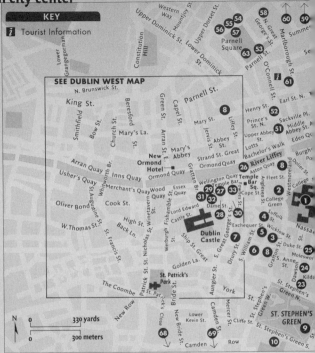

SEE DUBLIN WEST MAP

N

0 | 330 yards
0 | 300 meters

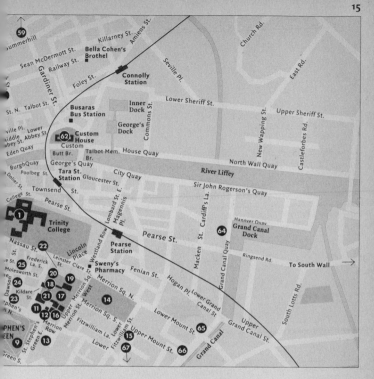

Summerhill

Killarney St.

Church Rd.

Sean McDermott St.

Bella Cohen's Brothel

Amiens St.

Railway St.

Seville Pl.

East Rd.

Foley St.

Gardiner St.

Connolly Station

St. N. Talbot St.

Lower Sheriff St.

Busaras Bus Station

Inner Dock

Upper Sheriff St.

George's Dock

Commons St.

New Wapping St.

Castleforbes Rd.

Custom House

Custom Br.

Talbot Mem. Br.

House Quay

North Wall Quay

Butt Br.

George's Quay

BurghQuay

Tara St. Station

City Quay

River Liffey

Poolbeg

Gloucester St.

Sir John Rogerson's Quay

Doler St.

Townsend St.

Pearse St.

Lombard St. E.

Magenni's Pl.

Macken St.

Cardiff's La.

College St.

Trinity College

Hanover Quay

Grand Canal Dock

Nassau St.

Lincoln Place

Pearse St.

Grand Canal Quay

Ringsend Rd.

To South Wall

Frederick La. S.

Leinster Clare St.

Westland Row

Pearse Station

Molesworth St.

Sweny's Pharmacy

Fenian St.

Hogan Pl.

Lower Grand Canal St.

Kildare St.

Merrion St. West

Merrion Sq. N.

Merrion Sq. E.

National Gallery of Ireland, 19

Upper Merrion St.

Lower Mount St.

Upper Grand Canal St.

South Lotts Rd.

Merrion Sq. S.

Fitzwilliam La.

Merrion St.

Green E.

Row

Lower Fitzwilliam St.

Upper Mount St.

Grand Canal

ST. STEPHEN'S GREEN

St. Stephen's

Lower Fitzwilliam

Green S.

William Street—it's one of Dublin's best haunts for the caffeine-addicted and its staff is devoid of the devil-may-care, pseudo-existential inefficiency that seems to plague so many other Dublin cafés. *78 Grafton St., tel. 01/677–6761 (for all locations except Great George's St.); Sun.–Thurs. 7:30 AM–1 AM, Fri.–Sat. 7:30 AM–4 AM. 13 Great George's St., tel. 01/679–2078; Mon.–Thurs. 7:45 AM–6 PM, Fri.–Sat. 7:45 AM–6 PM and 10:30 PM–4 AM. 12 Westmoreland St.; Mon.–Sat. 7:30 AM–9 PM, Sun. 9:30 AM–9 PM. 40 Mary St.; Mon.–Wed. and Fri.–Sat. 7 AM–6 PM, Thurs. 7 AM–9 PM.*

❻ DUBLIN CIVIC MUSEUM. Built between 1765 and 1771 as an exhibition hall for the Society of Artists, this building later was used as the City Assembly House, precursor of City Hall. The museum's esoteric collection includes Stone Age flints, Viking coins, old maps and prints of the city, and the sculpted head of British admiral Horatio Nelson, which used to top Nelson's Pillar, beside the General Post Office (☞ North of the Liffey, *below*) on O'Connell Street; the column was toppled by an explosion in 1966 on the 50th anniversary of the Easter Uprising. The museum holds exhibitions relating to the city. *58 S. William St., tel. 01/679–4260. Free. Tues.–Sat. 10–6, Sun. 11–2.*

❹ DUBLIN TOURISM. Churches are not just for prayers, as this deconsecrated medieval church proves. Resurrected as a visitor center, St. Andrew's, fallen into ruin after years of neglect, now houses Dublin Tourism, a private concern that offers the most complete information on Dublin's sights, restaurants, and hotels; you can even rent a car here. The office provides reservations facilities for all Dublin hotels, as well as guided tours, a plethora of brochures, and a gift shop (beware the exorbitant prices). Upstairs is a pleasant café serving sandwiches and drinks. *St. Andrew's Church, Suffolk St., tel. 01/605–7700 or 1850/230330 (within Ireland). July–Sept., Mon.–Sat. 8:30–6, Sun. 11–5:30; Oct.–June, daily 9–6.*

❼ GEORGE'S STREET ARCADE. This Victorian covered market fills the block between Drury Street to the west and South Great George's Street to the east. It's changed little, despite a restoration.

You'll find two dozen or so stalls selling books, prints, clothing (mostly secondhand), exotic foodstuffs, and trinkets. *S. Great George's St. Mon.–Sat. 9–6.*

NEED A
BREAK? One of Dublin's most ornate traditional taverns, the **Long Hall Pub** (51 S. Great George's St., tel. 01/475–1590) has Victorian lamps, a mahogany bar, mirrors, chandeliers, and plasterwork ceilings, all more than 100 years old. The pub serves sandwiches and an excellent pint of Guinness.

★ ❸ **GRAFTON STREET.** It's no more than 200 yards long and about 20 ft wide, but brick-lined Grafton Street, open only to pedestrians, can make a claim to be the most humming street in the city, if not in all of Ireland. It is one of Dublin's vital spines: the most direct route between the front door of Trinity College and Stephen's Green, and the city's premier shopping street, home to Dublin's two most distinguished department stores, **Brown Thomas** and **Marks & Spencer** (☞ Shopping). Both on Grafton Street itself and in the smaller alleyways that radiate off it, there are also dozens of independent stores, a dozen or so colorful flower sellers, and some of Dublin's most popular watering holes (☞ Nightlife and the Arts). In summertime, buskers from all over the country and the world line both sides of the street, pouring out the sounds of drum, whistle, pipe, and string.

❶❷ **HUGUENOT CEMETERY.** One of the last such burial grounds in Dublin, this cemetery was used in the late 17th century by French Protestants who had fled persecution in their native land. The cemetery gates are rarely open, but you can view the grounds from the street. It stands on the northeast corner across from the square. *27 St. Stephen's Green N.*

❶⓪ **NEWMAN HOUSE.** One of the greatest glories of Georgian Dublin, Newman House is actually two imposing town houses joined together. The earliest, No. 85 St. Stephen's Green (1738), was designed by Richard Castle, favored architect of Dublin's rich and famous, and features a winged Palladian window on the Wicklow granite facade. Originally known as Clanwilliam House, it features two landmarks of Irish Georgian style: the Apollo Room, decorated with stuccowork depicting the sun god and his muses; and the magnificent Saloon, "the supreme example of Dublin Baroque," according to scholars Jacqueline O'Brien and Desmond Guinness, crowned with an exuberant ceiling aswirl with cupids and gods, created by the Brothers Lafranchini, the finest *stuccadores* (plasterworkers) of 18th-century Dublin. Next door at No. 86 (1765), the staircase is one of the city's most beautiful rococo examples, with floral swags and musical instruments picked out in cake-frosting white on pastel-color walls. Catholic University (described by James Joyce in *A Portrait of the Artist as a Young Man*) was established in this building in 1850, with Cardinal John Henry Newman as its first rector. At the back of Newman House lie **Iveagh Gardens,** a delightful hideaway with statues and sunken gardens that remains one of Dublin's best-kept secrets (you can enter via Earlsfort Terrace and Harcourt Street). The Commons Restaurant (☞ Eating Out) is in the basement. *85–86 St. Stephen's Green, tel. 01/475–7255. £2. June–Aug., weekdays 9–5, but visitation limited to supervised tours, daily June–Aug. at noon, 2, 3, and 4 PM.*

⑤ POWERSCOURT TOWNHOUSE CENTRE. Lucky man, this Viscount Powerscourt. In the mid-18th century, not only did he build Ireland's most spectacular country house, in Enniskerry, County Wicklow (which bears the family name), but he also decided to rival that structure's grandeur with one of Dublin's largest stone mansions. Staffed with 22 servants and built of granite from the viscount's own quarry in the Wicklow Hills, Powerscourt House was a major statement in the Palladian style designed by Robert Mack in 1774— a massive, Baroque-style edifice that towers over the little street it sits on (note the top story, framed by massive volutes, that was once intended as an observatory). The interior decoration runs from rococo salons by James McCullagh to Adamesque plasterwork by Michael Stapleton to—surprise—an imaginative shopping atrium, installed in and around the covered courtyard. The stores here include high-quality Irish crafts shops and numerous food stalls (☞ Shopping). The mall exit leads to the Carmelite **Church of St. Teresa's** and **Johnson's Court**. Beside the church, a pedestrian lane leads onto Grafton Street. *59 S. William St. Mon.–Sat.*

⑬ RHA GALLAGHER GALLERY. The Royal Hibernian Academy, an old Dublin institution, is housed in a well-lit building, one of the largest exhibition spaces in the city. The gallery holds adventurous exhibitions of the best in contemporary art, both from Ireland and abroad. *15 Ely Pl. off St. Stephen's Green, tel. 01/661–2558. Free. Mon.–Wed. and Fri.–Sat. 11–5, Thurs. 11–9, Sun. 2–5.*

★ **⑪ SHELBOURNE MÉRIDIEN HOTEL.** The ebullient, redbrick, white wood-trimmed facade of the Shelbourne has commanded "the best address in Dublin" from the north side of St. Stephen's Green since 1865. In 1921 the Irish Free State's constitution was drafted here in a first-floor suite. The most financially painless way to soak up the hotel's old-fashioned luxury and genteel excitement is to step past the entrance—note the statues of Nubian princesses and attendant slaves—for afternoon tea (£13.50 per person, including sandwiches and cakes) in the green-wallpapered **Lord Mayor's Lounge** or for a drink in one of its two bars, the **Shelbourne Bar** and the **Horseshoe Bar** (☞ Nightlife and the Arts), both of which are thronged with businesspeople and politicos after the workday ends. Elizabeth Bowen, famed novelist, wrote her novel *The Hotel* about this very place. *27 St. Stephen's Green, tel. 01/676–6471. www.shelbourne.ie*

★ **⑨ ST. STEPHEN'S GREEN.** Dubliners call it simply Stephen's Green, and green it is (year-round)—a verdant, 27-acre city-center square that was an open common used for the public punishment of criminals until 1664. After a long period of decline, it became a private park in 1814—the first time in its history that it was closed to the general public. Its fortunes changed again in 1880, when Sir Arthur Guinness, later Lord Ardilaun (a member of the Guinness brewery family), paid for it to be laid out anew. Flower gardens, formal lawns, a Victorian bandstand, and an ornamental lake that is home to many waterfowl are all within the park's borders, connected by paths guaranteeing that strolling here or just passing through will offer up unexpected delights (be sure to look out for palm trees). Among the park's many statues are a memorial to Yeats and another to Joyce by Henry Moore, and the *Three Fates*, a dramatic group of bronze female figures watching over man's destiny. In the 18th century the walk on the north side of the green was referred to as the Beaux Walk because most of Dublin's gentlemen's clubs were in town houses here. Today it is dominated by the **Shelbourne Méridien Hotel** (☞ *above*). On the south side is another alluring attraction, Georgian-gorgeous Newman House (☞ *above*). *Free. Daily sunrise–sunset.*

★ ❶ **TRINITY COLLEGE.** Founded in 1592 by Queen Elizabeth I to "civilize" (Her Majesty's word) Dublin, Trinity is Ireland's oldest and most famous college. The memorably atmospheric campus is a must; here you can enjoy tracking the shadows of some of the more noted alumni, such as Jonathan Swift (1667–1745), Oscar Wilde (1854–1900), Bram Stoker (1847–1912), and Samuel Beckett (1906–89). Trinity College, Dublin (familiarly known as TCD) was founded on the site of the confiscated Priory of All Hallows. For centuries Trinity was the preserve of the Protestant church. A free education was offered to Catholics—provided that they accepted the Protestant faith. As a legacy of this condition, until 1966 Catholics who wished to study at Trinity had to obtain a dispensation from their bishop or face excommunication. Today more than 70% of Trinity's students are Catholics, an indication of how far away those days seem to today's generation.

Trinity's grounds cover 40 acres. Most of its buildings were constructed in the 18th and early 19th centuries. The extensive **West Front,** with a classical pedimented portico in the Corinthian style, faces College Green and is directly across from the **Bank of Ireland** (☞ *above*); it was built between 1755 and 1759, possibly the work of Theodore Jacobsen, architect of London's Foundling Hospital. The design is repeated on the interior, so the view is the same both from outside the gates and from the quadrangle inside. On the lawn in front of the inner facade are **statues** of orator Edmund Burke (1729–97) and dramatist Oliver Goldsmith (1728–74), two other alumni. Like the West Front, **Parliament Square** (commonly known as Front Square), the cobblestoned quadrangle that lies just beyond this first patch of lawn, also dates from the 18th century. On the right side of the square is Sir William Chambers's **theater,** or **Examination Hall,** dating from the mid-1780s, which contains the college's most splendid Adamesque interior (designed by Michael Stapleton). The hall houses an impressive organ retrieved from an 18th-century Spanish ship and a gilded oak chandelier from the old House of Commons; concerts are sometimes held here. The **chapel,** which stands on the left of the quadrangle, has stucco ceilings and fine woodwork. Both the theater and the chapel were designed by Scotsman William Chambers in the late 18th century. The looming **Campanile,** or bell tower, is the symbolic heart of the college; erected in 1853, it dominates the center of the square. To the left of the campanile is the **Graduates Memorial Building,** or GMB. Built in 1892, the slightly Gothic building is now home to both the Philosophical and Historical Societies, Trinity's ancient and fiercely competitive debating groups. At the back of the square stands old redbrick **Rubrics,** looking rather ordinary and out of place among the gray granite and cobblestones. Rubrics, now used as rooms for students and faculty, dates from 1690, making it the oldest building still standing.

Ireland's largest collection of books and manuscripts is housed in
★ **Trinity College Library.** Its principal treasure is the *Book of Kells*, generally considered the most striking manuscript ever produced in the Anglo-Saxon world and one of the greatest masterpieces of early Christian art. Once thought to be lost—the Vikings looted the book in 1007 for its jeweled cover but ultimately left the manuscript behind—the book is a splendidly illuminated version of the Gospels. In the 12th century, Guardius Cambensis declared that the book was made by an angel's hand in answer to a prayer of St. Bridget; in the 20th century, scholars decided instead that the book originated

on the island of Iona in Scotland, where followers of St. Colomba lived until the island came under siege in the early to mid-9th century. They fled to Kells, County Meath, bringing the book with them. The 680-page work was rebound in four volumes in 1953, two of which are usually displayed at a time, so you typically see no more than four original pages. (Some wags have taken to calling it the "Page of Kells.") However, such is the incredible workmanship of the Book of Kells that one folio contains the equivalent of many other manuscripts. On some pages, it has been determined that within a quarter inch, no fewer than 158 interlacements of a ribbon pattern of white lines on a black background can be discerned— little wonder some historians feel this book contains all the designs to be found in Celtic art. Note, too, the extraordinary colors, some of which were derived from shellfish, beetles' wings, and crushed pearls. The most famous page shows the "XPI" monogram (symbol of Christ), but if this page is not on display, you can still see a replica of it, and many of the other lavishly illustrated pages, in the adjacent exhibition—dedicated to the history, artistry, and conservation of the book—through which you must pass to see the originals.

Because of the fame and beauty of the Book of Kells, it is all too easy to overlook the other treasures in the library. They include the Book of Armagh, a 9th-century copy of the New Testament that also contains St. Patrick's Confession, and the legendary Book of Durrow, a 7th-century Gospel book from County Offaly. You may have to wait in line to enter the library; it's less busy early in the day.

The **Old Library,** aptly known as the Long Room, is one of Dublin's most staggering sights, at 213 ft long and 42 ft wide. It contains in its 21 alcoves approximately 200,000 of the 3 million volumes in Trinity's collection. Originally the room had a flat plaster ceiling, but in 1859–60 the need for more shelving resulted in a decision to raise the level of the roof and add the barrel-vaulted ceiling and the gallery bookcases. Since the 1801 Copyright Act, the college has received a copy of every book published in Britain and Ireland, and a great number of these publications must be stored in other parts of the campus and beyond. Of note are the carved Royal Arms of Queen Elizabeth I, above the library entrance—the only surviving relic of the original college buildings—and, lining the Long Room, a grand series of marble busts, of which the most famous is Roubiliac's portrait of Jonathan Swift. The **Trinity College Library Shop** sells books, clothing, jewelry, and postcards. *tel. 01/608–2308. £4.50. June–Sept., Mon.–Sat. 9:30–5, Sun. 9:30–4:30; Oct.–May, Mon.–Sat. 9:30–5, Sun. noon–4:30.*

Trinity College's stark, modern Arts and Social Sciences Building, with an entrance on Nassau Street, houses the **Douglas Hyde Gallery of Modern Art,** which concentrates on contemporary art exhibitions and has its own bookstore. Also in the building, down some steps from the gallery, there's a snack bar with coffee, tea, sandwiches, and students willing to talk about life in the old college. *tel. 01/608–1116. Free. Mon.–Wed. and Fri. 11–6, Thurs. 11–7, Sat. 11–4:45.*

The **New Berkeley Library,** the main student library at Trinity, was built in 1967 and named after the philosopher and alumnus George Berkeley. The small open space in front of the library contains a spherical brass sculpture designed by Arnaldo Pomodoro. The library is not open to the general public. *College Green, tel. 01/677–2941. Grounds daily 8 AM–10 PM.*

In the Thomas Davis Theatre in the arts building, the **"Dublin Experience"** is a 45-minute audiovisual presentation devoted to the history of the city over the last 1,000 years. *tel. 01/608–1688. £3; in conjunction with Old Library (☞ above), £6. May–Oct., daily 10–5; shows every hr on the hr.*

THE GEORGIAN HEART OF DUBLIN

If there's one travel poster that signifies "Dublin" more than any other, it's the one that pictures 50 or so Georgian doorways—door after colorful door, all graced with lovely fanlights upheld by columns. A building boom began in Dublin in the early 18th century, as the Protestant ascendancy constructed town houses for themselves and civic structures for their city in the style that came to be known as Georgian, for the four successive British Georges who ruled from 1714 through 1830. The Georgian architectural rage owed much to architects like James Gandon and Richard Castle. They and others were influenced by Andrea Palladio (1508–80), whose *Four Books of Architecture* were published in the 1720s in London and helped to precipitate the revival of his style that swept through England and its colonies. Never again would Dublin be so "smart," so filled with decorum and style, nor its visitors' book so full of aristocratic names. Note that while Dublin's southside is a veritable shop window of the Georgian style, there are many other period sights to be found northside—for instance, the august interiors of the Dublin Writers Museum and Belvedere College, or James Gandon's great civic structures, the Custom House and the Four Courts, found quayside. These, and other Georgian goodies, are described in the Exploring sections of Dublin West and North of the Liffey, *below.*

A Good Walk

When Dublin was transformed into a Georgian metropolis, people came from all over to admire the new pillared and corniced city. Today, walking through Fitzwilliam Square or Merrion Street Upper, you can still admire vistas of calm Georgian splendor. Begin your Palladian promenade at the northeast corner of Stephen's Green—here, in front of the men's clubs, was the Beaux Walk, a favorite 18th-century gathering place for fashionable Dublin. Chances are you won't bump into a duke on his way to a Handel concert or an earl on his way to a rout, ball, and supper, but then, you won't have to dodge pigs, which used to dot the cityscape back then. Walk down Merrion Street to **Merrion Square** ⑭—one of Dublin's most attractive squares. The east side of Merrion Square and its continuation, Fitzwilliam Street, form what is known as "the Georgian mile," which, unlike some Irish miles, in fact measures less than a kilometer. On a fine day the Dublin Mountains are visible in the distance and the prospect has almost (thanks to the ugly, modern office block of the Electricity Supply Board) been preserved to give an impression of the spacious feel of 18th-century Dublin. Walk down the south side of the square to **Number Twenty-Nine** ⑮. Cut back through the square to visit the refurbished **Government Buildings** ⑯, the **Natural History Museum** ⑰, **Leinster House** ⑱, and/or the **National Gallery of Ireland** ⑲. The last leg of this walk is up Kildare Street to the **National Library** ⑳, passing the back of Leinster House to the **National Museum** ㉑. Stop in at the **Genealogical Office** ㉒ if you're doing research about your ancestors. Walk back to Stephen's Green and down Dawson Street, which runs parallel to Grafton Street. The **Mansion House** ㉓, **Royal Irish Academy** ㉔, and **St. Ann's Church** ㉕ are on the left as you walk down toward Trinity College's side entrance.

TIMING

Dublin is so compact you could race through this walk in two hours, if you don't linger anywhere or set foot in one of the museums. But there are treasures galore at the National Gallery and the National Museum; the green tranquillity of Merrion Square; and many of Dublin's finest sites along the way (not to mention dozens of the city's most historic pubs)—so if you can, this is a good walk to do over the course of a half day.

Sights to See

㉒ **GENEALOGICAL OFFICE.** Are you a Fitzgibbon from Limerick, a Cullen from Waterford, or a McSweeney from Cork? This reference library is a good place to begin your ancestor-tracing efforts. If you're a total novice at genealogical research, you can meet with an advisor (£25 for an hour consultation) who can help get you started. It also houses the **Heraldic Museum** (weekdays 10–8:30, Sat. 10–12:30), where displays of flags, coins, stamps, silver, and family crests highlight the uses and development of heraldry in Ireland. *2 Kildare St., tel. 01/603–0200. Genealogical Office weekdays 10–4:30, Sat. 10–12:30. Free. Guided tours by appointment.*

16 **GOVERNMENT BUILDINGS.** The swan song of British architecture in the capital, this enormous complex was the last neoclassic edifice to be erected by the British government. A landmark of "Edwardian Baroque," it was designed by Sir Aston Webb—who did many of the similarly grand buildings in London's Piccadilly Circus—as the College of Science in the early 1900s. Following a major restoration in the early 1990s, these buildings became the offices of the Department of the *taoiseach* (the prime minister, pronounced *tea-shuck*) and the *tánaiste* (the deputy prime minister, pronounced tawn-ish-ta). Fine examples of contemporary Irish furniture and carpets now decorate the offices. A stained-glass window, known as "My Four Green Fields," was originally made by Evie Hone for the 1939 World Trade Fair in New York. It depicts the four ancient provinces of Ireland: Munster, Ulster, Leinster, and Connacht. The government offices are accessible only via 45-minute guided tours given on Saturday (tickets are available on the day of the tour from the National Gallery), though they are dramatically illuminated every night. *Upper Merrion St., tel. 01/662–4888. Free. Sat. 10:30–3:30.*

18 **LEINSTER HOUSE.** Built in 1745, Leinster House was commissioned by the Duke of Leinster and almost singlehandedly helped to ignite the Georgian style that dominated Dublin for 100 years. It was not only the largest private residence in the city but the first structure in Ireland by Richard Castle, a follower of Palladio, who was to design some of the country's most important Palladian country houses. Inside, the grand salons were ornamented with coffered ceilings, Rembrandts, and Van Dycks, fitting settings for the parties often given by the duke's wife, Lady Emily Lennox, a celebrated beauty. The building has two facades: the one facing Merrion Square is designed in the style of a country house; the other, on Kildare Street, is that of a town house. This latter facade—if you ignore the ground-floor level—was a major inspiration for Irishman James Hoban's designs for the White House in Washington, D.C. Built in hard Ardbracan limestone, the house's exterior makes a cold impression, and, in fact, the duke's heirs pronounced the house "melancholy" and fled. Today, the house is the seat of Dáil Éireann (the House of Representatives, pronounced dawl e-rin) and Seanad Éireann (the Senate, pronounced shanad e-rin), which together constitute the Irish Parliament. When the Dáil is not in session, tours can be arranged weekdays; when the Dáil is in session, tours are available only on Monday and Friday. The Dáil visitors' gallery is included in the tour, although it can be accessed on days when the Dáil is in session and tours are not available. To arrange a visit, contact the public relations office at the phone number provided. *Kildare St., tel. 01/618–3000.*

㉓ MANSION HOUSE. Home to the mayor of Dublin, the Mansion House dates from 1710, when it was built for Joshua Dawson, who later sold the property to the government on condition that "one loaf of double refined sugar of six pounds weight" be delivered to him every Christmas. In 1919 the Declaration of Irish Independence was adopted here. Dawson Street (named for the house's original tenant) is the site of the annual and popular **August Antiques Fair.** *Dawson St.*

★ ⑭ MERRION SQUARE. Created between 1762 and 1764, this tranquil square a few blocks to the east of St. Stephen's Green is lined on three sides by some of Dublin's best-preserved Georgian town houses, many of which have brightly painted front doors above which sit intricate fanlights. Leinster House—Dublin's Versailles—along with the Natural History Museum and the National Gallery line the west side of the square, but it is on the other sides that the Georgian terrace streetscape comes into its own, with the finest houses located on the north border. Even when its flower gardens are not in bloom, the vibrant, mostly evergreen grounds, dotted with sculpture and threaded with meandering paths, are worth a walk-through. The square has been the home of several distinguished Dubliners, including Oscar Wilde's parents, Sir William and "Speranza" Wilde (No. 1); Irish national leader Daniel O'Connell (No. 58); and authors W. B. Yeats (Nos. 52 and 82) and Sheridan LeFanu (No. 70). Walk past the houses and read the plaques on the house facades, which identify the former inhabitants. Until 50 years ago, the square was a fashionable residential area, but today most of the houses are offices. At the south end of Merrion Square, on Upper Mount Street, stands **St. Stephen's Church.** Known locally as the "pepper canister" church because of its cupola, the structure was inspired in part by Wren's churches in London. *Merrion Sq. Daily sunrise–sunset.*

★ **⑲ NATIONAL GALLERY OF IRELAND.** Caravaggio's *The Taking of Christ* (1602), Reynolds's *First Earl of Bellamont* (1773), Vermeer's *Lady Writing a Letter with Her Maid* (ca. 1670) . . . you get the picture. The National Gallery of Ireland—the first in a series of major civic buildings on the west side of Merrion Square—is one of Europe's finest smaller art museums, with more than 3,000 works. Unlike Europe's largest art museums, which are almost guaranteed to induce Stendhal's syndrome, the National Gallery can be thoroughly covered in a morning or afternoon without inducing exhaustion. An 1854 Act of Parliament provided for the establishment of the museum, which was helped along by William Dargan (1799–1867), who was responsible for building much of Ireland's railway network in the 19th century (he is honored by a statue on the front lawn). The 1864 building was designed by Francis Fowke, who was also responsible for London's Victoria & Albert Museum. More art than ever before is on display following the completion in 1996 of a four-year renovation and expansion.

A highlight of the museum is the major collection of paintings by Irish artists from the 17th through 20th centuries, including works by Roderic O'Conor (1860–1940), Sir William Orpen (1878–1931), William Leech (1881–1968), and Jack B. Yeats (1871–1957), the brother of W. B. Yeats and by far the best-known Irish painter of the 20th century. Yeats painted portraits and landscapes in an abstract expressionist style not dissimilar from that of the later Bay Area Figurative painters of the 1950s and 1960s. His *The Liffey Swim* (1923) is particularly worth seeing for its Dublin subject matter (the annual swim is still held, usually on the first weekend in September).

The collection also claims exceptional paintings from the 17th-century French, Dutch, Italian, and Spanish schools. Among the highlights that you should strive to see are those mentioned above (the spectacular Caravaggio made headlines around the world when it was found hanging undiscovered in a Jesuit house not far from the museum) and Rembrandt's *Rest on the Flight into Egypt* (1647), Poussin's *The Holy Family* (1649) and *Lamentation over the Dead Christ* (ca. 1655–60), and, somewhat later than these, Goya's *Portrait of Doña Antonia Zárate* (ca. 1810). Don't forget to check out the amazing portrait the *First Earl of Bellamont*, by Reynolds; the earl was among the first to introduce the Georgian fashion to Ireland and this portrait stunningly flaunts the extraordinary style of the man himself. The French Impressionists are represented with paintings by Monet, Sisley, and Pissarro. The northern wing of the gallery houses the British collection and the Irish National Portrait collection, and the amply stocked **gift shop** is a good place to pick up books on Irish artists. An addition on nearby Clare Street was to be completed by early 2001. Free guided tours are available on Saturday at 3 PM and on Sunday at 2:15, 3, and 4. *Merrion Sq. W, tel. 01/661–5133. Free. Mon.–Wed. and Fri.–Sat. 10–5:30, Thurs. 10–8:30, Sun. 2–5. www.nationalgallery.ie*

NEED A BREAK? **Fitzer's** (Merrion Sq. W, tel. 01/661–4496), the National Gallery's self-service restaurant, is a find—one of the city's best spots for an inexpensive, top-rate lunch. The 16–20 daily menu items are prepared with an up-to-date take on new European cuisine. It's open Thursday until 8 and Sunday 2–5 in addition to Monday–Saturday lunch.

⑰ **NATURAL HISTORY MUSEUM.** Dr. Stanley Livingstone inaugurated this museum when it opened in 1857. Today, it is little changed from Victorian times and remains a fascinating repository of mounted mammals, birds, and other flora and fauna. The most famous exhibits are the skeletons of Ireland's extinct, prehistoric giant "Irish elk" and the 65-ft whale skeleton suspended from the roof. The museum is next door to the ☞ **Government Buildings**. *Merrion Sq. W, tel. 01/677–7444. Free. Tues.–Sat. 10–5, Sun. 2–5.*

⓴ NATIONAL LIBRARY. Ireland is one of the few countries in the world where one can happily admit to being a writer. And few countries as geographically diminutive as Ireland have garnered as many recipients of the Nobel Prize for Literature. Along with works by W. B. Yeats (1923), George Bernard Shaw (1925), Samuel Beckett (1969), and Seamus Heaney (1995), the National Library contains first editions of every major Irish writer, including books by Jonathan Swift, Oliver Goldsmith, and James Joyce (who used the library as the scene of the great literary debate in *Ulysses*). In addition, of course, almost every book ever published in Ireland is kept here, as well as an unequaled selection of old maps and an extensive collection of Irish newspapers and magazines—more than 5 million items in all. The main **Reading Room** opened in 1890 to house the collections of the Royal Dublin Society. Beneath its dramatic domed ceiling, countless authors have researched and written their books over the years. *Kildare St., tel. 01/661–8811. Free. Mon. 10–9, Tues.–Wed. 2–9, Thurs.–Fri. 10–5, Sat. 10–1.*

★ **㉑ NATIONAL MUSEUM.** On the other side of Leinster House from the National Library, Ireland's National Museum houses a fabled collection of Irish artifacts, dating from 7000 BC to the present. The museum is organized around a grand rotunda and elaborately decorated, with mosaic floors, marble columns, balustrades, and fancy ironwork. It has the largest collection of Celtic antiquities in the world, including an array of gold jewelry, carved stones, bronze tools, and weapons. The Treasury collection, including some of the museum's most renowned pieces, is open on a permanent basis. Among the priceless relics on display are the 8th-century **Ardagh Chalice,** a two-handle silver cup with gold filigree ornamentation; the bronze-coated, iron **St. Patrick's Bell,** the oldest surviving example (5th–8th centuries) of Irish metalwork; the 8th-century **Tara Brooch,** an intricately decorated piece made of white bronze, amber, and glass; and the 12th-century bejeweled oak **Cross of Cong,** covered with silver and bronze panels. The Road to Independence Room is devoted to the 1916 Easter Uprising and the War of Independence (1919–21); displays here include uniforms, weapons, banners, and a piece of the flag that flew over the General Post Office during Easter Week, 1916. Upstairs is a permanent exhibit on the Vikings, featuring a full-size Viking skeleton, swords, leather works recovered in Dublin and surrounding areas, and a replica of a small Viking boat. In contrast to the ebullient late-Victorian architecture of the main museum building, the design of the **National Museum Annexe** is purely functional; it houses temporary shows of Irish antiquities. The 18th-century **Collins Barracks** (☞ Phoenix Park and Environs, *below*), the most recent addition to the museum, houses the collection of glass, silver, furniture, and other decorative arts. *Kildare St.; Annexe: 7–9 Merrion Row; tel. 01/677–7444. Free. Tues.–Sat. 10–5, Sun. 2–5.*

⓯ NUMBER TWENTY-NINE. Everything in this carefully refurbished 1794 home, known simply as Number Twenty-Nine, is in keeping with the elegant lifestyle of the Dublin middle class between 1790 and 1820, the height of the Georgian period, when the house was owned by a wine merchant's widow. From the basement to the attic, in the kitchen, nursery, servant's quarters, and the formal living areas, the National Museum of Ireland has re-created the period's style with authentic furniture, paintings, carpets, curtains, paint, wallpapers, and even bellpulls. *29 Lower Fitzwilliam St., tel. 01/702–6165. £2.50. Tues.–Sat. 10–5, Sun. 2–5.*

㉔ ROYAL IRISH ACADEMY. Adjacent to the **Mansion House** (☞ *above*), the country's leading learned society houses important manuscripts in its 18th-century library, including a large collection of ancient Irish manuscripts such as the 11th–12th century *Book of the Dun Cow* and the library of the 18th-century poet Thomas Moore. *19 Dawson St., tel. 01/676–2570. Free. Weekdays 9:30–5.*

㉕ ST. ANN'S CHURCH (Church of Ireland). St. Ann's plain, neo-Romanesque, granite exterior, erected in 1868, belies the church's rich Georgian interior, designed in 1720 by Isaac Wills. Among the highlights of the interior are polished-wood balconies, ornate plasterwork, and shelving in the chancel dating from 1723 and still in use for the distribution of bread to the poor of the parish. *Dawson St. Free. Weekdays 10–3 and Sun. for services.*

TEMPLE BAR: DUBLIN'S "LEFT BANK"

More than anywhere else in Dublin, it is Temple Bar that represents the dramatic changes (good and bad) and ascending fortunes of Dublin in the 1990s. Named after one of the streets of its central spine, the area was targeted for redevelopment in 1991–92 after a long period of neglect, having survived widely rumored plans to turn it into a massive bus depot and/or a giant parking lot. Temple Bar took off—*fast*—into Dublin's version of New York's SoHo, Paris's Bastille, London's Notting Hill: a thriving mix of high and alternative culture distinct from that in every other part of the city. Dotting the area's narrow cobblestone streets and pedestrian alleyways are new apartment buildings (inside they tend to be small and uninspired, with sky-high rent), vintage-clothing stores, postage-stamp-size boutiques selling £200 sunglasses and other expensive gewgaws, art galleries galore, a hotel resuscitated by U2, hip restaurants, pubs, clubs, European-style cafés, and a smattering of cultural venues.

Temple Bar's regeneration was no doubt abetted by that one surefire real estate asset: location, location, location. The area is bordered by Dame Street to the south, the Liffey to the north, Fishamble Street to the west, and Westmoreland Street to the east. In fact, Temple Bar is so perfectly situated between everywhere else in Dublin that it's difficult to believe this neighborhood was once largely forsaken. It's now sometimes called the "playing ground of young Dublin," and for good reason: on weekend evenings and daily in the summer it teems with young people—not only from Dublin but from all over Europe—who fly into the city for the weekend, drawn by its pubs, clubs, and lively *craic*. It has become a favorite of young Englishmen on "stag" weekends,

48-hour bachelor parties heavy on drinking and debauching. Some who have witnessed Temple Bar's rapid gentrification and commercialization complain that it's losing its artistic soul— *Harper's Bazaar* said it was in danger of becoming "a sort of pseudoplace," like London's Covent Garden Piazza or Paris's Les Halles. Over the next few years the planned Smithfield development (☞ North of the Liffey, *below*) may replace Temple Bar at the cutting edge of Dublin culture, but for the moment there's no denying that this is one of the best places to get a handle on the city.

A Good Walk

Start at O'Connell Bridge and walk down Aston Quay, taking in the terrific view west down the River Liffey. Alleys and narrow roads to your left lead into Temple Bar, but hold off turning in until you get to **Ha'penny Bridge** ㉖, a Liffey landmark. Turn right and walk through Merchant's Arch, the symbolic entry into Temple Bar (see if you can spot the surveillance cameras up on the walls), which leads you onto the area's long spine, named Temple Bar here but also called Fleet Street (to the east) and Essex Street (both east and west, to the west). You're right at Temple Bar Square, one of the two largest plazas in Temple Bar. Just up on the right are two of the area's leading art galleries, the Temple Bar Gallery (at Lower Fownes Street) and, another block up, the Original Print Gallery and Black Church Print Studio (☞ Nightlife and the Arts). Turn left onto Eustace Street. If you have children, you may want to go to the **Ark** ㉗, a children's cultural center. Across the street from the Ark, stop in at the Temple Bar Information Centre (☞ Practical Information) and pick up a handy *Temple Bar Guide*. Farther down Eustace Street is the **Irish Film Centre** ㉘, Temple Bar's leading cultural venue and a great place to catch classic or new indie films. In summer, the IFC organizes Saturday-night outdoor screenings on **Meeting House Square** ㉙, behind the Ark, accessed via Curved Street. The street is dominated on one side by the **Arthouse** ㉚ and on the other by the Temple Bar Music Centre (☞ Nightlife and the Arts). Dublin's leading photography gallery, the **Gallery of Photography** ㉛, is also here. Walk a few steps west to the narrow, cobbled Sycamore Street, and then turn right and walk to Dame Street, where you'll find the **Olympia Theatre** ㉜. Farther down Dame Street, the ultramodern **Central Bank** ㉝ rises above the city. Head for the corner of Parliament Street, where you can stop for a break or begin the next walk.

TIMING

You can easily breeze through Temple Bar in an hour or so, but if you've got the time, plan to spend a morning or afternoon here, drifting in and out of its dozens of stores and galleries, relaxing at a café over a cup of coffee or at a pub over a pint, maybe even seeing a film if you're looking for a change from sightseeing.

Sights to See

🖑 ㉗ **THE ARK.** If you're traveling with children and looking for something fun to do, be sure to stop by the Ark, Ireland's children's cultural center, housed in a former Presbyterian church. Its theater opens onto Meeting House Square for outdoor performances in summer. A gallery and workshop space host ongoing activities. *Eustace St., tel. 01/670–7788. Free. Weekdays 9:30–4, Sat. 10–4.*

㉚ **ARTHOUSE.** This is one of the first purpose-built multimedia centers for the arts in the world. Its modern design—all glass, metal, and painted concrete—is the work of esteemed architect Shay Cleary Doyle, who intended the building to reflect the object glorified within: the computer. Inside is a training center, a performance venue, a creative studio, and an exhibition space that plays host to a variety of art exhibitions. Pride of place, however, goes to the Art Information Bureau and the Artifact artist's database, featuring the work of more than 1,000 modern Irish artists working in Ireland and abroad. This useful catalog is open to anyone wishing to buy or admire the work of the listed artists, and it is set up in such a way that you can search for work according to specific criteria; just press a few buttons and a list of artists and images of their work fitting your description will appear. An Internet café, Cyberia, is on the top floor. *Curved St., tel. 01/605–6800. Free. Weekdays 9:30–6.*

㉝ CENTRAL BANK. Designed by Sam Stephenson in 1978, the controversial, ultramodern, glass and concrete building suspends huge concrete slabs around a central axis. Skateboarders and in-line skaters have taken up residence on the little plaza in front of the building. *Dame St., tel. 01/671–6666. Free. Weekdays 10–6.*

㉛ GALLERY OF PHOTOGRAPHY. Dublin's premier photography gallery has a permanent collection of early 20th-century Irish photography and also puts on monthly exhibits of contemporary Irish and international photographers. The bookstore is the best place in the city to browse for photography books and pick up arty postcards. *Meeting House Sq. S, tel. 01/671–4654. Free. Mon.–Sat. 11–6.*

㉖ HA'PENNY BRIDGE. This heavily trafficked footbridge crosses the Liffey at a prime spot: Temple Bar (☞ *above*) is on the south side, and the bridge provides the fastest route to the thriving Mary and Henry Street shopping areas to the north (☞ *Shopping*). Until early in the 20th century, a half-penny toll was charged to cross it. Yeats was one among many Dubliners who found this too high a price to pay—more a matter of principle than of finance—and so made the detour via O'Connell Bridge. Congestion on the bridge has been relieved with the opening of the Millennium Footbridge a few hundred yards up the river.

㉘ IRISH FILM CENTRE (IFC). The opening of the IFC in a former Quaker meetinghouse in 1992 helped to launch the revitalization of Temple Bar. It has two comfortable art-house cinemas showing revivals and new independent films, the Irish Film Archive, a bookstore for cineastes, and a "happening" bar, all of which make this one of the neighborhood's most vital cultural institutions. *6 Eustace St., tel. 01/679–5744. Free. Weekdays 9:30–late, weekends 11–late.*

NEED A BREAK? The creamiest, frothiest coffees in all of Temple Bar can be had at the **Joy of Coffee/Image Gallery Café** (25 E. Essex St., Temple

Bar, tel. 01/679–3393); the wall of windows floods light onto the small gallery with original photographs adorning the walls.

29 MEETING HOUSE SQUARE. Behind the Ark (☞ *above*) and accessed via Curved Street, Meeting House Square has become something of a gathering place for Dublin's youth and artists. Throughout the summer, seats are erected and a wide variety of events—including classic movies (every Saturday night), theater, games, and family programs—are held here. It's also a favorite site for the continuously changing street sculpture that pops up all over Temple Bar. All year round it's a great spot to sit and relax and engage in a bit of people-watching. It hosts an organic food market every Saturday morning. The square gets its name from a nearby Quaker meetinghouse.

★ **32 OLYMPIA THEATRE.** One of the best places anywhere in Europe to see live musical acts, the Olympia is Dublin's second oldest and one of its busiest theaters. Built in 1879, this classic Victorian music hall has a gorgeous red wrought-iron facade. Conveniently, two pubs are situated through doors directly off the back of the theater's orchestra section. The Olympia's long-standing Friday and Saturday series, "Midnight at the Olympia," has brought a wide array of musical performers to Dublin, and the theater has also seen many notable actors strut its stage, including Alec Guinness, Peggy Ashcroft, Noël Coward, and even Laurel and Hardy. In November 1996, when Van Morrison played Dublin, he chose to perform here rather than in a larger venue. If you have a chance to catch a favorite performer (or to discover someone new), go!—you won't regret it. *72 Dame St., tel. 01/677–7744.*

NEED A BREAK? The trendy **Irish Film Centre Café** (6 Eustace St., tel. 01/679–5744) is a surprisingly pleasant place for a lunchtime break. Sandwiches are large and healthy, with plenty of nonmeat choices, and the people-watching is nonpareil.

DUBLIN WEST: FROM DUBLIN CASTLE TO THE FOUR COURTS

This section of Dublin takes you from the 10th-century crypt at Christ Church Cathedral—the city's oldest surviving structure—to the modern plant of the Guinness Brewery. It also crosses the Liffey for a visit to Smithfield, the old market area being billed as the next hot location in the city. Dublin is so compact, however, that to separate the following sites from those covered in the two other city-center southside walks is misleading, suggesting that this area is removed from the heart of the city center. In fact, this tour's starting point, City Hall, is just across the street from Thomas Read's, and Christ Church Cathedral is a very short walk farther west. However, the westernmost sites covered here—notably the Royal Hospital and Kilmainham Gaol—*are* at some distance, more so than may be comfortable if you're not an enthusiastic walker, so you may want to drive or catch a cab or a bus out to them.

A Good Walk

Begin with a brief visit to **City Hall** ㉞, and then walk up Cork Hill to the Castle Street entrance to **Dublin Castle** ㉟, whose highlights—the grand salons that show off Viceregal Dublin at its most splendid—are only visitable via a guided tour. The castle is also the new home of the **Chester Beatty Library** ㊱, a world-renowned collection of Oriental art. Leave via the same gate, turn left, and walk up Castle Street to ancient **Christ Church Cathedral** ㊲, picturesquely situated on one of the few hills in the city. At the southeast corner of the cathedral, connected via an utterly beguiling Victorian-era bridge, **Dublinia** ㊳ gives you a chance to experience life in medieval Dublin. And just down Nicholas Street is—begorrah!—**St. Patrick's Cathedral** ㊴. If you're eager to venture back to the 17th century or love old books, visit the quaint **Marsh's Library** ㊵, next door to St. Patrick's. You can then stroll through the old artisan redbrick dwellings in the Liberties, home to the heaviest concentration of the city's antiques stores, to Thomas Street and—just follow your nose—the **Guinness Brewery** ㊶, where you can keep your spirits up in more ways than one. At this point, if you want to see more architecture and modern art, proceed farther west to the Irish Museum of Modern Art in the elegant 18th-century **Royal Hospital Kilmainham** ㊷, and the **Kilmainham Gaol** ㊸. If you don't elect to head this way, turn back down Thomas Street, crossing the Liffey at Bridge Street, which on its north side becomes Church Street. On your left is the **Four Courts** ㊹. A little farther up on the left is **St. Michan's Church** ㊺ and the beginning of the Smithfield area, which includes the brand-new **Ceol** ㊻, a museum dedicated to traditional Irish music. A quick jog over to Bow Street (via Mary's Lane) brings you to the **Old Jameson Distillery** ㊼—here you'll learn all there is to learn about Irish whiskey.

TIMING

Allow yourself a few hours, especially if you want to include the Guinness Brewery and the Irish Museum of Modern Art at the Royal Hospital. Keep in mind that if you want to cover the easternmost sites—Dublin Castle, City Hall, Christ Church Cathedral, and environs—you can easily append them onto a tour of Temple Bar.

Sights to See

★ ☝ ㊻ **CEOL.** At the heart of the new Smithfield Village development is Chief O'Neill's complex, consisting of a hotel (☞ Where to Stay) and Ceol, a new interactive museum of Irish music. The museum tells the ancient story of Celtic music in a thoroughly modern fashion. The History of Irish Music area consists of five rooms dedicated to different periods from the age of myth and legend to the present. Computerized exhibits allow you to pick and choose as much detail as you want. The Stories Room contains a priceless oral history of musicians and storytellers from early in the last century. The Song Room illustrates the centuries-old Irish love of lyrics, from the haunting, unaccompanied sean nós style to the scatological Dublin ballad. The four major instruments of Irish music—fiddle, flute, button accordion, and *uilleann* (elbow) pipes (small, bellow-blown bagpipes played sitting down)—are displayed on the ground floor. Throughout the museum, touch screens allow access to recordings of the masters of the genre plus hundreds of film clips of them performing. A children's area has an ingenious game of musical twister that allows kids to play along with a tune, using parts of their body to play the notes. *Smithfield Village, tel. 01/ 817–3820. £3.75. Mon.–Sat. 9:30–6. www.ceol.ie*

㊱ CHESTER BEATTY LIBRARY. Formerly in the suburb of Ballsbridge, the library is now housed in the clock tower building of **Dublin Castle** (☞ *below*). Sir Alfred Chester Beatty (1875–1968), a Canadian mining millionaire, assembled one of the most significant collections of Islamic and Far Eastern art in the Western world, which he then donated to Ireland. Among the library's exhibits are clay tablets from Babylon dating from 2700 BC, Japanese color wood-block prints, Chinese jade books, and Turkish and Persian paintings. It also has 250 manuscripts of the Koran from throughout the Moslem world. Guided tours of the library are available on Tuesday and Saturday at 2:30 PM. *Castle St., tel. 01/269–2386. Free. Tues.–Fri. 10–5, Sat. 2–5.*

★ ㊲ CHRIST CHURCH CATHEDRAL. You'd never know from the outside that the first Christianized Danish king built a wooden church at this site in 1038; thanks to the extensive 19th-century renovation of its stonework and trim, the cathedral looks more Victorian than Anglo-Norman. Construction on the present Christ Church—the flagship of the Church of Ireland and one of two Protestant cathedrals in Dublin (the other is St. Patrick's just to the south; ☞ *below*)—was begun in 1172 by Strongbow, a Norman baron and conqueror of Dublin for the English crown, and went on for 50 years. By 1875 the cathedral had deteriorated badly, so a major renovation gave it much of the look it has today, including the addition of one of Dublin's most charming structures: a Bridge of Sighs–like affair that connects the cathedral to the old Synod Hall, which now holds the Viking extravaganza, Dublinia (☞ *below*). Remains from the 12th-century building include the north wall of the nave, the west bay of the choir, and the fine stonework of the transepts, with their pointed arches and

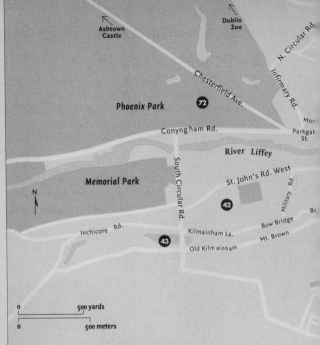

Aughrim St.

Ircular Rd.

Upper Grange

Phibsborough

Western Way

Mountjoy

Western Way

Upper Dominick St.

Lower Dorset St.

O'Connell St.

Brunswick St.

King St.

Church St.

Parnell St.

Green St.

Mary St.

Jervis St.

Capel St.

O'Connell St.

70

Arbour Hill

Rd.

Montpelier Hill

Parkgate St.

71

Benburb St.

Wolfe Tone Quay

Ellis Quay

Arran Quay

Smithfield

47

Bow St.

45

Mary's La.

Abbey St.

O'Connell Br.

Strand St.

Ormond Quay

River Liffey

Aston Quay

Fleet St.

Sean Heuston Br.

Victoria Quay

Ushers Island

Ushers Quay

St. Augustine St.

44

Inns Quay

Winetavern St.

37

Dame St.

36

34

Bow La. W.

James's St.

41

Oliver Bond

W. Thomas

50

High St.

49

Cook St.

Castle St.

35

Dublin Castle

Ship St. Gt.

Great Georges St.

Crane St.

St. Francis St.

38

St. Nicolas St.

48

Golden Ln.

Patrick's Close

St. Patrick's Park

39

The Coombe

40

supporting columns. Strongbow himself is buried in the cathedral beneath an impressive effigy. The vast, sturdy **crypt,** with its 12th- and 13th-century vaults, is Dublin's oldest surviving structure and the building's most notable feature. *Christ Church Pl. and Winetavern St., tel. 01/677–8099. £2. Daily 9:30–5.*

③④ CITY HALL. Facing the Liffey from Cork Hill at the top of Parliament Street, this grand Georgian municipal building (1769–79), once the Royal Exchange, was designed by Thomas Cooley and marks the southwestern corner of Temple Bar. Today it's the seat of the Dublin Corporation, the elected body that governs the city. Twelve columns encircle the domed central rotunda, which has a fine mosaic floor and 12 frescoes depicting Dublin legends and ancient Irish historical scenes. Just off the rotunda is a gently curving staircase, a typical feature of most large Dublin town houses. *Cork Hill, tel. 01/679–6111 ext. 2807. Free. Weekdays 9–1 and 2:15–5.*

③⑤ DUBLIN CASTLE. Neil Jordan's film *Michael Collins* captured Dublin Castle's near-indomitable status well: seat and symbol of the British rule of Ireland for 7¼ centuries, the castle figured largely in Ireland's turbulent history early in the 20th century. After extensive renovations, it's now used mostly for Irish and EU governmental purposes. The sprawling **Great Courtyard** is the reputed site of the Black Pool (Dubh Linn, pronounced *dove*-lin) from which Dublin got its name, though today it is lined with stretch limos and security guards. In the Lower Castle Yard, the **Record Tower,** the earliest of several towers on the site, is the largest remaining relic of the original Norman buildings, built by King John between 1208 and 1220. The clock tower building now houses the **Chester Beatty Library** (☞ *above*). Guided tours are available around the principal **State Apartments** (on the southern side of the Upper Castle Yard), formerly the residence of the English viceroys. Now used by the president of Ireland to host visiting heads of state and EU ministers, they are lavishly furnished with rich Donegal carpets and illuminated by Waterford glass chandeliers. The largest and most impressive of these chambers, **St. Patrick's Hall,** with its gilt pillars and painted ceiling, is used for the inauguration of Irish presidents. The **Round Drawing Room,** in Bermingham Tower, dates from 1411 and was rebuilt in 1777; a number of Irish leaders were imprisoned in the tower, from the 16th century to the early 20th century. The blue oval **Wedgwood Room** contains Chippendale chairs and a marble fireplace. The **Castle Vaults** now holds an elegant little patisserie and bistro.

On the grounds of the castle is the **Church of the Holy Trinity** (formerly called Chapel Royal), designed in 1814 by Francis Johnston, who also designed the original General Post Office building on O'Connell Street. Carved oak panels and stained glass depicting viceroys' coats of arms grace the interior. Look up to view the elaborate array of fan vaults that decorates the ceiling. On the outside more than 100 carved heads adorn the walls. St. Peter and Jonathan Swift preside over the north door, St. Patrick and Brian Boru over the east. One-hour guided tours of the castle are available every half hour, but the rooms are closed when in official use, so phone first. The easiest way in to the castle today is via the **Cork Hill Gate,** just west of City Hall. *Castle St., tel. 01/677–7129. State Apartments £3, including tour. Weekdays 10–5, weekends 2–5.*

🐚 **38** **DUBLINIA.** In the old Synod Hall (formerly a meeting place for bishops of the Church of Ireland), attached via a covered stonework Victorian bridge to **Christ Church Cathedral** (☞ *above*), Dublin's Medieval Trust has set up an entertaining and informative reconstruction of everyday life in medieval Dublin. The main exhibits use high-tech audiovisual and computer displays; there are also a scale model of what Dublin was like around 1500, a medieval maze, a life-size reconstruction based on the 13th-century dockside at Wood Quay, and a fine view from the tower. For a more modern take on the city, study the noted James Malton series of prints of 18th-century Dublin hanging on the walls of the coffee shop. *St. Michael's Hill, tel. 01/679–4611. Exhibit £3.95. Apr.– Sept., daily 10–5; Oct.–Mar., Mon.–Sat. 11–4, Sun. 10–4:30.*

44 **FOUR COURTS.** Today the seat of the High Court of Justice of Ireland, the Four Courts are James Gandon's second Dublin masterpiece, built between 1786 and 1802, close on the heels of his **Custom House** (☞ *below*), downstream on the same side of the River Liffey. The Four Courts replaced a 13th-century Dominican abbey that stood here earlier. In 1922, during the Irish Civil War, the Four Courts was almost totally destroyed by shelling, and the adjoining Public Records Office was gutted, with many of its priceless legal documents destroyed, including innumerable family records; efforts to restore the building to its original state spanned 10 years. Today the stately Corinthian portico and the circular central hall are well worth viewing. Its distinctive copper-covered dome atop a colonnaded rotunda makes this one of Dublin's most instantly recognizable buildings; the view from the rotunda is terrific. Although there is no tour of the building, you are welcome to sit in while the courts are in session. *Inns Quay, tel. 01/872–5555. Daily 10–1 and 2:15–4.*

★ ㊶ **GUINNESS BREWERY.** Founded by Arthur Guinness in 1759, Ireland's all-dominating brewer—in fact, at one stage the largest stout-producing brewery in the world—is on a 60-acre spread west of Christ Church Cathedral. It happens to be the most popular tourist destination in town—not surprisingly, since the Irish national drink is Guinness stout, a dark brew made with roasted malt. If you're used to lighter, lager-type beers you may find this rich dark concoction, with its thick creamy "head" or "collar," somewhat unusual at first taste. But once the taste is acquired, it soon becomes an addiction. The brewery itself is closed to the public, but the 19th-century **Hop Store,** on Crane Street, part museum and part gift shop, puts on an 18-minute audiovisual presentation. The show ends with the curtain rising on the kind of old-fashioned pub—with mahogany decor, mirrors, and snugs—that is fast becoming hard to find in modern Dublin. You then receive two complimentary glasses (or one pint) of the famous black stout (a smile and a polite request might get you a couple more). The Guinness Zone, an interactive exhibit on the second floor, highlights the history of the beer's remarkably successful advertising campaigns, from the famous "Guinness is Good for You" poster ads to the ultrasleek television commercials of the present day. A gift shop sells the best of Guinness memorabilia: posters, bar towels, beer mats, and garments. *James' Gate, tel. 01/453–3645. £4. Daily 9:30–5. www.guinness.com*

43 KILMAINHAM GAOL. Even farther west than the Royal Hospital, this is a grim, forbidding structure where leaders of the 1916 Easter Uprising, including Pádrig Pearse and James Connolly, were held before being executed in the prison yard. In the 19th century, other inmates here were the revolutionary Robert Emmet and Charles Stewart Parnell, a leading politician. You can visit the cells, a chilling sight, while the guided tour and a 30-minute audiovisual presentation relate a graphic account of Ireland's political history over the past 200 years from a Nationalist viewpoint. You can only visit the prison as part of a guided tour, which leaves every hour on the hour. There is also a small tearoom on the premises. *Inchicore Rd., tel. 01/453–5984. £3. Apr.–Sept., daily 9:30–5; Oct.– Mar., weekdays 9:30–4, Sun. 10–5.*

40 MARSH'S LIBRARY. A short walk west from St. Stephen's Green and accessed through a tiny but charming cottage garden lies a gem of old Dublin: the city's—and Ireland's—first public library, founded and endowed in 1701 by Narcissus Marsh, the Archbishop of Dublin, then open to "All Graduates and Gentlemen." The two-story, brick, Georgian building has been practically unchanged inside since it was built. It houses a priceless collection of 250 manuscripts and 25,000 16th- to 18th-century books. Many of these rare volumes are locked inside cages, as are the readers who wish to peruse them. The cages were to discourage students who, often impecunious, may have been tempted to make the books their own. The library has been restored with great attention to its original architectural details, especially in the book stacks. *St. Patrick's Close off Patrick St., tel. 01/454–3511. £1. Mon. and Wed.–Fri. 10–12:45 and 2–5, Sat. 10:30–12:45.*

47 OLD JAMESON DISTILLERY. Founded in 1791, this distillery produced one of Ireland's most famous whiskeys for nearly 200 years until 1966, when local distilleries merged to form Irish Distillers and moved to a purpose-built, ultramodern distillery in Middleton, County Cork. Part of the complex was converted into the group's head office, and the distillery itself was turned into a museum. You can watch a short audiovisual history of the industry, which actually had its origins 1,500 years ago in Middle Eastern perfume making, and tour the old distillery, where you can learn about the distilling of whiskey from grain to bottle. You can also view a reconstruction of a former warehouse, where the colorful nicknames of former barrel makers are recorded. There's a 20-minute audiovisual show, a 40-minute tour, and a complimentary tasting (remember: Irish whiskey is best drunk without a mixer—try it straight or with water); four attendees are invited to taste different brands of Irish whiskey and compare them against bourbon and Scotch. If you have a large group and everyone wants to do this, phone in advance to arrange it. *Bow St., tel. 01/807–2355. Tour £3.95. Daily 9:30–5:30; tours every ½ hr.*

★ **42 ROYAL HOSPITAL KILMAINHAM.** A short ride by taxi or bus from the city center, this replica of Les Invalides in Paris is regarded as the most important 17th-century building in Ireland. Commissioned as a hospice for disabled and veteran soldiers by James Butler, the Duke of Ormonde and Viceroy to King Charles II, it was completed in 1684, making it the first classical building in the city and a precursor of Dublin's golden age. It survived into the 1920s as a hospital, but after the founding of the Irish Free State in 1922, the building fell into disrepair. Over the last 15 years or so, restoration has returned the entire edifice to what it once was.

The structure consists of four galleries around a courtyard and includes a grand dining hall, 100 ft long by 50 ft wide. The architectural highlight is the hospital's Baroque **chapel,** distinguished by its extraordinary plasterwork ceiling and fine wood carvings. "There is nothing in Ireland from the 17th century that can come near this masterpiece," raves cultural historian John FitzMaurice Mills. Today the Royal Hospital houses the **Irish Museum of Modern Art.** The museum displays works by non-Irish, 20th-century greats like Picasso and Miró but concentrates on the work of Irish artists. Richard Deacon, Richard Gorman, Dorothy Cross, Sean Scully, Matt Mullican, Louis Le Brocquy, and James Colman are among the contemporary Irish artists represented. The Café Musée has soups, sandwiches, and other light fare. *Kilmainham La., tel. 01/612–9900. Royal Hospital free, but individual shows may have separate charges; Museum of Modern Art permanent collection free, small charge for special exhibitions. Royal Hospital Tues.– Sat. 10–5:30, Sun. noon–5:30, tour every ½ hr; Museum of Modern Art Tues.–Sat. 10–5:30, Sun. noon–5:30; tours Wed. and Fri. 2:30, Sat. 11:30. www.modernart.ie*

45 **ST. MICHAN'S CHURCH.** Built in 1685 on the site of an older, 11th-century Danish church (Michan is a Danish saint), this Anglican church is architecturally undistinguished except for its 120-ft-high bell tower. But its 18th-century organ was supposedly played by Handel for his first-ever performance of the *Messiah*, and its Stool of Repentance is the only one still in existence in the city; parishioners who were judged to be "open and notoriously naughty livers" used it to do public penance. St. Michan's main claim to notoriety, however, is down in the vaults, where the totally dry atmosphere has preserved a number of corpses in a remarkable state of mummification. They lie in open caskets, and if you're strong-hearted, you can shake hands with a former religious crusader or nun! Most of the preserved bodies are thought to have been Dublin tradespeople. *Lower Church St., tel. 01/872–4154. £2. Weekdays 10–12:45 and 2–4:45, Sat. 10–12:45, Sun. service at 10 AM.*

39 **ST. PATRICK'S CATHEDRAL.** The largest cathedral in Dublin and also the national cathedral of the Church of Ireland, St. Patrick's is the second of the capital's two Protestant cathedrals (the other is Christ Church; ☞ *above*). (The reason that Dublin has two cathedrals is that St. Patrick's originally stood outside the walls of Dublin, while its close neighbor was within the walls and belonged to the see of Dublin.) Legend has it that St. Patrick baptized many converts at a well on the site of the cathedral in the 5th century. The original building, dedicated in 1192 and early English Gothic in style, was an unsuccessful attempt to assert supremacy over Christ Church Cathedral. At 305 ft, it is the longest church in the country, a fact that Oliver Cromwell's troops—no friends to the Irish—found useful, as they made the church's nave into their stable in the 17th century. Their visit left the building in a ruinous state, and its current good repair is largely due to the benevolence of Sir Benjamin Guinness, of the brewing family, who started to finance major restoration work in 1860. Be sure to view the gloriously heraldic **Choir of St. Patrick's,** hung with colorful medieval banners, as well as find the tomb of the most famous of St. Patrick's many illustrious deans, Jonathan Swift, immortal author of *Gulliver's Travels,* who held office from 1713 to 1745. **Swift's tomb** is in the south aisle, not far from that of his beloved "Stella," Mrs. Esther Johnson. Swift's epitaph is inscribed over the robing-room door. Yeats—who translated it thus: "Swift has sailed into his rest; Savage indignation there cannot lacerate his breast"—declared it the greatest epitaph of all time. Other memorials include the 17th-century **Boyle Monument,** with its numerous painted figures of family members, and the **monument to Turlough O'Carolan,** the last of the Irish bards and one of the country's finest harp players. To the immediate north of the cathedral is a small park, with statues of many of Dublin's literary figures and **St. Patrick's Well.** Matins (9:45 AM) and evensong (5:35 PM) are still sung on most days, a real treat for the music lover. *Patrick St., tel. 01/475–4817. £2. May and Sept.–Oct., weekdays 9–6, Sat. 9–5, Sun. 10–11 and 12:45–3; June–Aug., weekdays 9–6, Sat. 9–4, Sun. 9:30–3 and 4:15–5:15; Nov.–Apr., weekdays 9–6, Sat. 9–4, Sun. 10–11 and 12:45–3.*

THE LIBERTIES

A stroll through the Liberties is a walk through working-class Dublin, past and present, good and bad. The name derives from Dublin of the Middle Ages, when the area south and west of Christ Church Cathedral was outside the city walls and free from the jurisdiction of the city rulers. A certain amount of freedom, or "liberty," was enjoyed by those who settled here, and it often attracted people on the fringes of society, especially the poor.

A Good Walk

Start on Patrick Street, in the shadow of St. Patrick's Cathedral. Look down the street toward the Liffey and a glorious view of Christ Church. Take a right on Dean Street, where you'll find John Fallons pub. Take a right off Dean Street onto Francis Street and walk uphill. A number of quality antiques shops (☞ Shopping) line both sides of the thoroughfare. Halfway up Francis Street, on the right, behind hefty wrought-iron gates, is one of Dublin's most-overlooked treasures, **St. Nicholas of Myra's Church** ㊽. Continue up Francis Street and take the next right onto Thomas Davis Street (named after a famous patriot and revolutionary—the Liberties has long had a close association with Irish Nationalism). The street is full of classic, two-story redbrick houses. The area, once the heart of "Darlin' Dublin" and the holy source of its distinctive accent, is rapidly becoming yuppified. Back on Francis Street, in an old factory building with its chimney stack intact, is the exciting **Iveagh Market Hall** ㊾. At the top of Francis Street turn left onto Thomas Street. Across the road, on your right side, stands the wonderfully detailed exterior of St. Augustine and St. John, with its grandiose spire dominating the area around. You'll notice churches all over the Liberties; the bishops thought it wise to build holy palaces in the poorest areas of the city as tall, shining beacons of comfort and hope. Farther up Thomas Street in another converted factory is the **National College of Art and Design** ㊿.

TIMING

Unless you intend on doing some serious antiques shopping, this is a relatively quick stroll—perhaps two hours—as the Liberties is a compact area of small, winding streets.

Sights to See

49 IVEAGH MARKET HALL. One of numerous buildings bestowed upon the city of Dublin by Lord Iveagh of the Guinness family, the cavernous, Victorian, redbrick-and-granite Iveagh Market Hall holds a regular, eclectic market from Tuesday to Saturday. *Francis St., Tues.–Sat. 9–5.*

50 NATIONAL COLLEGE OF ART AND DESIGN. The delicate welding of glass and iron onto the redbrick Victorian facade of this onetime factory makes this school worth a visit. Walk around the cobblestone central courtyard, where there's always the added bonus of viewing some of the students work in mediums such as glass, clay, metal, and stone. *Thomas St., tel. 01/671–1377.*

48 ST. NICHOLAS OF MYRA'S CHURCH. This church was completed in 1834 in grand neoclassic style. Inside, the highly ornate chapel includes ceiling panels of each of the 12 apostles and a pietà raised 20 ft above the marble altar, which is guarded on each side by angels sculpted by John Hogan while he was in Florence. The tiny nuptial chapel to the right has a small Harry Clarke stained-glass window. *St. Nicholas St. Free. Hrs vary.*

NORTH OF THE LIFFEY

If you stand on O'Connell Bridge or the pedestrian-only Ha'penny span, you'll get excellent views up and down the Liffey, the *abha na life*, which James Joyce transcribed phonetically as Anna Livia in *Finnegan's Wake*. Here, framed with embankments just like those along Paris's Seine, the river is near the end of its 128-km (80-mi) journey from the Wicklow Mountains into the Irish Sea.

And near here, you begin a pilgrimage into James Joyce Country and the fascinating sights of Dublin's northside.

Today the northside—a mix of densely thronged shopping streets and run-down sections (though the property boom is rapidly refurbishing these areas) of once-genteel homes—absolutely warrants a walk for three reasons: its major cultural institutions (which include the Gate Theatre, the James Joyce Cultural Centre, the Dublin Writers Museum, and the Hugh Lane Municipal Gallery of Modern Art), the number of sites of significance with ties to Irish Republicanism, and its busy streets. During the 18th century, most of the upper echelons of Dublin society lived in the Georgian houses around Mountjoy Square and shopped along Capel Street, which was lined with stores stocking fine furniture and silver. The construction of Merrion Square on the southside (completed in 1764) and nearby Fitzwilliam Square (completed in 1825), and the decision by Ireland's grandest duke to build Leinster House on the southside, permanently changed the northside's fortunes. The city's fashionable social center crossed the Liffey, and although some of the northside's illustrious inhabitants clung to their houses, this area gradually became more run-down. The northside's fortunes may be changing, though. Once-derelict swaths of houses, especially on and near the Liffey, are being rehabilitated, and a large new shopping center opened on Mary Street in late 1996. Now a huge shopping mall and entertainment complex are planned for O'Connell Street, right where the defunct Cartlon Cinema stands. Still, the redevelopment that has swept through Temple Bar is only in its early stages here, but precisely because it's a place on the cusp of transition, it's an interesting part of town to visit.

A Good Walk

Begin at O'Connell Bridge—if you look closely at it you will notice that it is wider than it is long—and head north up **O'Connell Street** ⑤. Stop to admire the monument to Daniel O'Connell, "The

Liberator," erected as a tribute to the great orator's achievement in securing Catholic Emancipation in 1829 (note the obvious scars from the fighting of 1916 on the figures). Then continue north to the **General Post Office** ⑤, a major site in the Easter Uprising of 1916. O'Connell leads to the southeastern corner of Parnell Square. Heading counterclockwise around the square, you'll pass in turn the **Gate Theatre** ㉝ and **Abbey Presbyterian Church** ㉞ before coming to the **Dublin Writers Museum** ㉟ and the **Hugh Lane Municipal Gallery of Modern Art** ㊱, both on the north side of the square and both housed in glorious neoclassic mansions; these are the two sites where you should plan to spend most of your time on the northside. Either before you go in or after you come out, you might want to visit the solemn yet serene **Garden of Remembrance** ㊲.

From here, you have two choices: to continue exploring the cultural sights that lie to the northeast of Parnell Square and east of O'Connell Street or to head to Moore, Henry, and Mary streets for a flavor of middle-class Dublin that you won't get on the spiffier southside. If you decide to continue your cultural explorations, jump two blocks northeast of Parnell Square to the **James Joyce Cultural Centre** ㊳, then head farther northeast to the once-glamorous **Mountjoy Square** ㊴. From here, turn south, stopping in at the **St. Francis Xavier Church** ㊵ on Gardiner Street. Head back west to Marlborough Street (parallel to and between Gardiner and O'Connell streets) to visit the **Pro-Cathedral** ㊶. Continue down to the quays and jog a block east to the **Custom House** ㊷. If you decide to shop with the locals, leave Parnell Square via the southwestern corner, stopping first to check out the chapel at the **Rotunda Hospital** ㊸. Moore Street is your first left off Parnell Street and leads directly to Henry Street.

TIMING
The northside has fewer major attractions than the southside and, overall, is less picturesque. As a result, you're unlikely to want

to stroll as leisurely here. If you zipped right through this walk, you could be done in less than two hours. But the two major cultural institutions covered here—the Dublin Writers Museum and the Hugh Lane Municipal Gallery of Modern Art—easily deserve several hours each, so it's worth doing this walk only if you have the time to devote to them.

Sights to See

54 ABBEY PRESBYTERIAN CHURCH. A soaring spire marks the exterior of this church, popularly known as Findlater's Church, after Alex Findlater, a noted Dublin grocer who endowed it. Completed in 1864, the church stands on the northeast corner of Parnell Square; the inside has a stark Presbyterian atmosphere, despite stained-glass windows and ornate pews. For a bird's-eye view, take the small staircase that leads to the balcony. *Parnell Sq. Free. Hrs vary.*

62 CUSTOM HOUSE. Seen at its best reflected in the waters of the Liffey during the short interval when the high tide is on the turn, the Custom House is the city's most spectacular Georgian building. Extending 375 ft on the north side of the river, this is the work of James Gandon, an English architect who arrived in Ireland in 1781, when construction commenced (it continued for 10 years). Crafted from gleaming Portland stone, the central portico is linked by arcades to the pavilions at either end. Too bad the dome is on the puny side and out of proportion. A statue of Commerce tops the graceful copper dome; statues on the main facade are based on allegorical themes. Note the exquisitely carved lions and unicorns supporting the arms of Ireland at the far ends of the facade. Republicans set the building on fire in 1921, but it was completely restored and now houses government offices. The building opened to the public in mid-1997 after having been closed for many years, and with it came a new exhibition tracing the building's history and significance.

Custom House Quay, tel. 01/679–3377. £1.50. Weekdays 9:30–5, weekends 2–5.

★ **⑤⑤ DUBLIN WRITERS MUSEUM.** "If you would know Ireland—body and soul—you must read its poems and stories," wrote Yeats in 1891. Further investigation into the Irish way with words can be found here at this unique museum, set within a magnificently restored 18th-century town house on the north side of Parnell Square. Once the home of John Jameson (of the Irish whiskey family), the mansion is centered on an enormous drawing room, gorgeously decorated with paintings, Adamesque plasterwork, and a deep Edwardian lincrusta frieze. Rare manuscripts, diaries, posters, letters, limited and first editions, photographs, and other mementoes commemorate the life and works of the nation's greatest writers (and there are *many* of them, so leave plenty of time), including Joyce, Shaw, J. M. Synge, Lady Gregory, Yeats, Beckett, and many others. On display are an 1804 edition of Swift's *Gulliver's Travels*, an 1899 first edition of Bram Stoker's *Dracula*, and an 1899 edition of Wilde's *Ballad of Reading Gaol*. There's even a special "Teller of Tales" exhibit showcasing Behan, O'Flaherty, and O'Faolan. Readings are periodically held. The bookshop and café make this an ideal place to spend a rainy afternoon. If you lose track of time and stay until the closing hour, you might want to dine at Chapter One, a highly regarded restaurant in the basement (☞ Eating Out), which would have had Joyce ecstasizing about its currant-sprinkled scones. 18 Parnell Sq. N, tel. 01/872–2077. £3. June–Aug., Mon.–Sat. 10–6, Sun. 11–5; Sept.–May, Mon.–Sat. 10–5, Sun. 11–5.

⑤⑦ GARDEN OF REMEMBRANCE. Opened in 1966, 50 years after the Easter Uprising of 1916, the garden, within Parnell Square, commemorates all those who died fighting for Irish freedom. A large plaza is at the garden's entrance; steps lead down to the fountain area, graced with a sculpture by contemporary Irish artist Oisín Kelly based on the mythological Children of Lír, who were turned into swans. The garden serves as an oasis of tranquillity in the middle of the busy city. Parnell Sq. Daily 9–5.

GATE THEATRE. The Gate has been one of Dublin's most important theaters since its founding in 1929 by Micháel MacLiammóir and Hilton Edwards, who also founded Galway City's An Taibhdhearc as the national Irish-language theater. Many innovative productions by Irish playwrights have been staged here, and Dublin audiences have encountered foreign playwrights and actors here as well, including Orson Welles (his first paid performance) and James Mason, who also performed here early in his career. The show actually begins as soon as you walk into the auditorium—a Georgian masterwork designed by Richard Johnston in 1784 as an assembly room for the Rotunda Hospital complex. Today the theater plays it safe with a major repertory of European and American drama and new plays by established Irish writers. *Cavendish Row, tel. 01/874–4045.*

GENERAL POST OFFICE. Known as the GPO, it is one of the great civic buildings of Dublin's Georgian era, but its fame derives from the role it played during the Easter Uprising. It has an impressive facade in the neoclassic style and was designed by Francis Johnston and built by the British between 1814 and 1818 as a center of communications. This gave it great strategic importance and was one of the reasons why it was chosen by the insurgent forces in 1916 as a headquarters. Here, on Easter Monday, 1916, the Republican forces, about 2,000 in number, and under the guidance of Pádrig Pearse and James Connolly, stormed the building and issued the Proclamation of the Irish Republic. After a week of shelling, the GPO lay in ruins; 13 rebels were ultimately executed (including Connolly, who was dying of gangrene from a leg shattered in the fighting and had to be propped up in a chair before the firing squad). Most of the original building was destroyed, though the facade survived (you can still see the scars of bullets on the its pillars). Rebuilt and subsequently reopened in 1929, it is still a working post office, with an attractive two-story main concourse. A bronze sculpture depicting the dying Cuchulainn, a leader of the Red Branch

Knights in Celtic mythology, sits in the front window. The 1916 Proclamation and the names of its signatories are inscribed on the green marble plinth. *O'Connell St., tel. 01/872–8888. Mon.–Sat. 8–8, Sun. 10:30–6.*

★ ❻ **HUGH LANE MUNICIPAL GALLERY OF MODERN ART.** Built originally as a town house for the Earl of Charlemont in 1762, this residence was so grand its Parnell Square street was nicknamed "Palace Row" in its honor. Designed by Sir William Chambers (who also built the Marino Casino for Charlemont) in the best Palladian manner, its delicate and rigidly correct facade, extended by two demilune arcades, was fashioned from the "new" white Ardmulcan stone (now seasoned to gray). Charlemont was one of the cultural locomotives of 18th-century Dublin—his walls were hung with Titians and Hogarths, and he frequently dined with Oliver Goldsmith and Sir Joshua Reynolds—so he would undoubtedly be delighted that his home is now the Hugh Lane Gallery, named after a nephew of Lady Gregory (Yeats's aristocratic patron). Lane collected both Impressionist paintings and 19th-century Irish and Anglo-Irish works. A complicated agreement with the National Gallery in London (reached after heated diplomatic dispute) stipulates that a portion of the 39 French paintings amassed by Lane shuttle back and forth between London and here. You can see Pissarro's *Printemps,* Manet's *Eva Gonzales,* Morisot's *Jour d'Été,* and, the jewel of the collection, Renoir's *Les Parapluies.*

Between the collection of Irish paintings in the **National Gallery of Ireland** (☞ *above*) and the superlative works on view here, you can quickly become familiar with Irish 20th-century art. Irish artists represented here include Roderic O'Conor, well known for his views of the West of Ireland; William Leech, including his *Girl with a Tinsel Scarf* (ca. 1912) and *The Cigarette;* and the most famous of the group, Jack B. Yeats (W. B.'s brother). The museum has a dozen of his paintings, including *Ball Alley* (ca. 1927) and *There Is No Night* (1949). There is also strikingly displayed stained-glass work by early 20th-century Irish master artisans Harry Clarke and

Evie Hone. *Parnell Sq. N, tel.* 01/874–1903. *Free. Sept.–Mar., Tues.–Thurs.* 9:30–6, *Fri.–Sat.* 9:30–5, *Sun.* 11–5; *Apr.–Aug., Tues.–Wed.* 9:30–6, *Thurs.* 9:30–8, *Fri.–Sat.* 9:30–5, *Sun.* 11–5. *www.hughlane.ie*

58 **JAMES JOYCE CULTURAL CENTRE.** Not everyone in Ireland has read James Joyce, but everyone has heard of him—especially since a copy of his censored and suppressed *Ulysses* was one of the top status symbols of the early 20th century. Today, of course, Joyce is acknowledged to be one of the greatest modern authors, and his *Dubliners, Finnegan's Wake,* and *A Portrait of the Artist as a Young Man* can even be read as poetic "travel guides" to Dublin. Now open to the general public, this restored, 18th-century Georgian town house, once the dancing academy of Professor Denis J. Maginni, is a center for Joycean studies and events related to the author. It has an extensive library and archives, exhibition rooms, a bookstore, and a café. Along with housing the **Joyce Museum** in Sandycove, the center is the main organizer of "Bloomstime," which marks the week leading up to June 16's Bloomsday celebrations. *35 N. Great George's St., tel.* 01/878–8547. £2.75. *Mon.–Sat.* 9:30–5, *Sun.* 12:30–5.

59 **MOUNTJOY SQUARE.** Built over the two decades before 1818, this square was once surrounded by elegant, terraced houses, but today only the northern side remains intact. The once-derelict southern side has been restored and converted into apartments. Irishman Brian Boru, who led his soldiers to victory against the Vikings in the Battle of Clontarf in 1014, was said to have pitched camp before the confrontation on the site of Mountjoy Square. Playwright Sean O'Casey once lived here at No. 35 and used the square as a setting for *The Shadow of a Gunman.*

51 **O'CONNELL STREET.** Dublin's most famous thoroughfare, 150 ft wide, was previously known as Sackville Street, but its name was changed in 1924, two years after the founding of the Irish Free State. After the devastation of the 1916 Easter Uprising, the street had to be almost entirely reconstructed, a task that took until the end of the 1920s. The main attraction of the street, **Nelson's Pillar,** a Doric column towering over the city center and a marvelous vantage point, was blown up in 1966, the 50th anniversary of the Easter Uprising. The large **monument** at the south end of the street is dedicated to Daniel O'Connell (1775–1847), "The Liberator," and was erected in 1854 as a tribute to the orator's achievement in securing Catholic Emancipation in 1829. Seated winged figures represent the four "Victories,"—courage, eloquence, fidelity, and patriotism—all exemplified by O'Connell. Ireland's four ancient provinces—Munster, Leinster, Ulster, and Connacht— are identified by their respective coats of arms. Look closely and you'll notice that O'Connell is wearing a glove on one hand, as he did for much of his adult life, a self-imposed penance for shooting a man in a duel. Alongside O'Connell is another noted statue, a modern rendition of Joyce's **Anna Livia,** seen as a lady set within a waterfall and now nicknamed by the natives the "floozy in the Jacuzzi." **O'Connell Bridge,** the main bridge spanning the Liffey (wider than it is long), marks the street's southern end.

NEED A BREAK? You have a number of good alternatives for a break on the northside. One of Dublin's oldest hotels, the **Gresham** (Upper O'Connell St., tel. 01/874–6881), is a pleasant old-fashioned spot for a morning coffee or afternoon tea. **Conway's** (Parnell St. near Upper O'Connell St., tel. 01/873–2687), founded in 1745, is reputed to be Dublin's second-oldest pub. For a real Irish pub lunch, stop in at **John M. Keating** (14 Mary St. and 23 Jervis St., tel. 01/873–1567), at the corner of Mary and Jervis streets; head upstairs, where you can sit at a low table and chat with locals.

61 **PRO-CATHEDRAL.** Dublin's principal Catholic cathedral (also known as St. Mary's) was built between 1816 and 1825. Although the severely classical church design is on a suitably epic scale, the building was never granted full cathedral status, nor has the identity of its architect ever been discovered; the only clue is in the church ledger, which lists a "Mr. P." as the builder. The church's facade, with a six-Doric-pillared portico, is based on the Temple of Theseus in Athens; the interior is modeled after the Grecian-Doric style of St-Philippe du Roule in Paris. A Palestrina choir, in which the great Irish tenor John McCormack began his career, sings in Latin here every Sunday at 11. *Marlborough St., tel. 01/874–5441. Free. Daily 8–6.*

63 ROTUNDA HOSPITAL. Founded in 1745 as the first maternity hospital in Ireland or Britain, the Rotunda was designed on a grand scale by architect Richard Castle (1690–1751), with a three-story tower and a copper cupola. It's now most worth a visit for its **chapel,** with elaborate plasterwork executed by Bartholomew Cramillion between 1757 and 1758, appropriately honoring motherhood. The **Gate Theatre** (☞ *above*), in a lavish Georgian assembly room, is also part of the complex. *Parnell St., tel. 01/873–0700.*

60 ST. FRANCIS XAVIER CHURCH. One of the city's finest churches in the classical style, the Jesuit St. Francis Xavier's was begun in 1829, the year of Catholic Emancipation, and was completed three years later. The building is designed in the shape of a Latin cross, with a distinctive Ionic portico and an unusual coffered ceiling. The striking, faux-marble high altarpiece, decorated with lapis lazuli, came from Italy. The church appears in James Joyce's story "Grace." *Upper Gardiner St., tel. 01/836–3411. Free. Daily 7 AM–8:30 PM.*

ALONG THE GRAND CANAL

At its completion in 1795, the 547-km (342-mi) Grand Canal was celebrated as the longest in Britain and Ireland. It connected Dublin to the River Shannon, and horse-drawn barges carried cargo (mainly turf) and passengers to the capital from all over the country. By the mid-19th century the train had arrived and the great waterway slowly fell into decline, until the last commercial traffic ceased in 1960. But the 6-km (4-mi) loop around the capital is ideal for a leisurely stroll.

A Good Walk

Begin by walking down the Pearse Street side of Trinity College until you arrive at the Ringsend Road Bridge. Raised on stilts above the canal is the **Waterways Visitors Centre** ⑭. Head west along the bank until you reach the **Mount Street Bridge** ⑮. On the southside is Percy Place, a street with elegant, three-story, terraced houses. On the northside, a small lane leads up to the infamous **Scruffy Murphy's** ⑯ pub. Taking a little detour at the next right, you'll pass a road that leads up to St. Stephen's (☞ *above*). Another right takes you into Powerscourt, a classic, inner-city estate of two-up, two-down terraced houses. Return to the canal and continue your walk along Herbert Place. You can get really close to the dark green water here as it spills white and frothy over one of the many wood-and-iron locks (all still in working order) that service the canal. James Joyce lost his virginity to a prostitute on the next stretch of the Canal, around Lower Baggot Street Bridge, but these banks belong to the lonesome ghost of another writer, Patrick Kavanagh. A life-size **statue of Patrick Kavanagh** ⑰ sits here, contemplative, arms folded, legs crossed on a wooden bench. Less than a mile past Kavanagh's statue the canal narrows as it approaches Richmond Bridge. Just beyond the bridge is the **Irish Jewish Museum** ⑱. To finish your walk in style, take a right onto Richmond Street, past a few antiques stores, until you arrive at **Bambrick's** ⑲, a public house in the best tradition of Dublin.

TIMING

You could walk this section of the canal in half an hour if you hurried, but what's the point? A leisurely pace best suits a waterside walk, so give yourself a couple of hours to visit the Jewish Museum and explore the old streets off the canal.

Sights to See

69 BAMBRICK'S. This is a pub in the best Irish tradition: a long, dark-wood bar, half-empty, frequented mostly by men over 50, with a staff whose sharp, grinning humor borders on being rude.

68 IRISH JEWISH MUSEUM. Though Ireland has never had a large Jewish population (it hovers around 1,800 today), in the late 19th century and early 20th century it did become home to roughly 5,000 European Jews fleeing the pogroms of Eastern Europe. Opened in 1985 by Israeli president Chaim Herzog (himself Dublin-educated), the museum has a restored synagogue and a display of photographs, letters, and personal memorabilia culled from Dublin's most prominent Jewish families, though the exhibits trace the Jewish presence in Ireland back to 1067. In homage to Leopold Bloom, the Jewish protagonist of Joyce's *Ulysses*, every Jewish reference in the novel has been identified. The museum is a 20-minute walk or so from St. Stephen's Green. *3–4 Walworth Rd., tel. 01/453–1797. Free. Oct.–Apr., Sun. 10:30–2:30; May–Sept., Tues., Thurs., and Sun. 11–3:30. Also by appointment.*

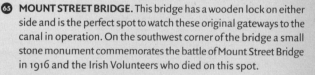

65 MOUNT STREET BRIDGE. This bridge has a wooden lock on either side and is the perfect spot to watch these original gateways to the canal in operation. On the southwest corner of the bridge a small stone monument commemorates the battle of Mount Street Bridge in 1916 and the Irish Volunteers who died on this spot.

66 SCRUFFY MURPHY'S. Many a backroom deal by the country's political power brokers has been made in the back room of this classy wood-and-brass pub. It's the perfect spot for a pint and a snack.

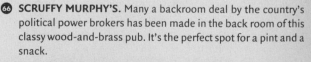

67 STATUE OF PATRICK KAVANAGH. Patrick Kavanagh, Ireland's great lyric poet, spent the later years of his life sitting on a bench here writing about the canal, which flowed from his birthplace in the Midlands to the city where he would die. In one such poem he tells those who outlive him, "O commemorate me with no hero-

courageous tomb, just a canal-bank seat for the passerby."
Acknowledging Kavanagh's devotion to this spot, his friends
commissioned a life-size bronze of the poet here. *Canal bank
along Wilton Terr.*

64 **WATERWAYS VISITORS CENTRE.** In the airy, wood-and-glass
building you can learn about the history of Irish rivers and canals
through photos, videos, and models. *Grand Canal Quay, tel. 01/677–
7501. £2. June–Sept., daily 9:30–6:30; Oct.–May, Wed.–Sun. 12:30–5.*

PHOENIX PARK AND ENVIRONS

Far and away Dublin's largest park, Phoenix Park (the name is an
anglicization of the Irish *Fionn Uisce*, meaning clear water) is a vast,
green arrowhead-shape oasis north of the Liffey, a 20-or-so-
minute walk from the city center. Today—Heaven send what
weather it may—Dubliners flock here to "take it aisy." It remains
the city's main lung, escape valve, sports center (cricket, soccer,
Gaelic games, and polo), and home to the noble creatures of the
Dublin Zoo. A handful of other cultural sites near the park are also
worth visiting, but to combine a visit to any of them with any of
our other walks would be a bit difficult. Ceol and the Old Jameson
Distillery, at the end of the Dublin West walk (☞ *above*), are the
sites closest (the Guinness Brewery (☞ *above*), across the river,
is also fairly close). So if you do make it to any of those, be sure
to evaluate whether you have enough time to append a visit to
one or another of these sites. Otherwise, plan to make a special
trip out here, either walking or going by car or cab.

A Good Walk

Beginning at the Custom House, walk down the quays on the north
side of the Liffey until you come to Blackhall Place. Walk up to
Arbour Hill and turn left: the **Arbour Hill Cemetery** 70 will be on
your left. Directly across Arbour Hill are the **Collins Barracks** 71,
now a branch of the National Museum (the main entrance is on
Benburb Street on the south side). On its east side Benburb

becomes Parkgate Street, and it's just a short stroll farther down to the main entrance of **Phoenix Park** ⑦.

TIMING
Phoenix Park is *big*; exploring it on foot could easily take the better part of a day. If you're looking for a little exercise, head here: jogging, horseback riding, and bicycling (☞ Outdoor Activities and Sports) are the ideal ways to explore the park more quickly than you can simply by strolling.

Sights to See

⑦⓪ **ARBOUR HILL CEMETERY.** A total of 14 Irishmen were executed by the British following the 1916 Easter Uprising. They were all buried here, including Pádrig Pearse, who led the rebellion; his younger brother Willie, who played a minor role in the uprising; and James Connolly, a socialist and labor leader wounded in the battle. Too weak from his wounds to stand, Connolly was tied to a chair and then shot. The burial ground is a simple but formal area, with the names of the dead leaders carved in stone beside an inscription of the proclamation they issued during the uprising. *Arbour Hill. Free. Mon.–Sat. 9–4:30, Sun. 9:30–noon.*

⑦① **COLLINS BARRACKS.** Until fairly recently, this was the oldest purpose-built military barracks in the world still in use. Now it's home to the National Museum's collection of glass, silver, furniture, and other decorative arts, exhibitions on Irish military history, and an exhibition of 200 years of Irish costumes and jewelry. *Benburb St., tel. 01/677–7444. Free. Tues.–Sat. 10–5, Sun. 2–5.*

★ ✋ ⑦② **PHOENIX PARK.** Europe's largest public park, extending about 5 km (3 mi) along the Liffey's north bank, encompasses 1,752 acres of verdant green lawns, woods, lakes, and playing fields. It's a jogger's paradise, but Sunday is the best time for everyone to visit: games of cricket, soccer, polo, baseball, hurling—a combination of lacrosse, baseball, and field hockey—and Irish football are likely to be in progress. Old-fashioned gas lamps line both sides of

Chesterfield Avenue, the main road that bisects the park for 4 km (2½ mi), which was named for Lord Chesterfield, a lord lieutenant of Ireland, who laid out the road in the 1740s. To the right as you enter the park, the **People's Garden** is a colorful flower garden designed in 1864.

Among the park's major monuments are the **Phoenix Column,** erected by Lord Chesterfield in 1747, and the **198-ft obelisk,** built in 1817 to commemorate the Duke of Wellington, the Irish general who defeated Napoleon for the British. (Wellington was born in Dublin but, true to the anti-Irish prejudice so prevalent in 19th-century England, balked at the suggestion that he was Irish: "If a man is born in a stable, it doesn't mean he is a horse," he is reputed to have said.) A tall **white cross** marks the spot where Pope John Paul II addressed more than a million people during his 1979 visit to Ireland. Wild deer can be seen grazing in the many open spaces of the park, especially near here.

You're guaranteed to see wildlife at the **Dublin Zoo,** the third-oldest public zoo in the world, founded in 1830, and just a short walk beyond the People's Garden (☞ *above*). The place looks a little dilapidated, but the government has allocated money for a five-year renovation that is now under way. Many animals from tropical climes are housed in barless enclosures, while Arctic species swim in the lakes close to the reptile house. The zoo is one of the few places in the world where lions will breed in captivity. Some 700 lions have been bred here since the 1850s, one of whom became familiar to movie fans the world over when MGM used him for its trademark. (As they will tell you at the zoo, he is in fact yawning in that familiar shot: an American lion had to be hired to roar and the "voice" was dubbed.) The children's corner has goats, guinea pigs, and lambs. In summer, the Lakeside Café serves ice cream and drinks. *Phoenix Park, tel. 01/677–1425. £6. Apr.–Oct., Mon.–Sat. 9:30–6, Sun. 10:30–6; Nov.–Mar., weekdays 9:30–4, Sat. 9:30–5, Sun. 10:30–5.*

Both the president of Ireland and the U.S. ambassador have official residences in the park (the president's is known as Aras an Uachtarain), but neither building is open to the public. The Garda Siochana (police) has its headquarters in the park; a small **Garda Museum** contains many relics of Irish police history, including old uniforms. *Phoenix Park, tel. 01/677–1156 ext. 2250. Free. Weekdays 9–5; call to confirm.*

Also within the park is a **visitor center,** in the 17th-century fortified Ashtown Castle; it has information about the park's history, flora, and fauna. *Phoenix Park, tel. 01/677–0095. £1.50. Mar.–May, daily 10–1 and 2–5; June–Sept., daily 9:30–6:30; Oct., daily 2–5; Nov.–Feb., weekends 9:30–4:30.*

NEED A BREAK? Just before the entrance to Phoenix Park, **Ryan's Pub** (28 Parkgate St., tel. 01/677–6097) is one of Dublin's last remaining genuine, late-Victorian-era pubs.

In This Chapter

Revised by Orna Mulcahy

eating out

ONCE UPON A TIME, and it wasn't too long ago, dining out in Dublin was a limited pleasure. Even 10 years ago, the city had lots of pubs but few interesting restaurants. All that has changed in recent years. With the Irish economy booming, everyone wants to eat out, and, not surprisingly, the Dublin dining scene has exploded with dazzling new places. Growing international interest and a more diverse local palate have also widened the range of restaurants and triggered new developments in Irish cuisine. So if you arrive thinking you're going to be eating potatoes, potatoes, and more potatoes, be prepared to have your preconceptions overturned—and to be very happily sated.

Many Dublin restaurateurs have trained in top restaurants in France, Switzerland, and Germany; others have worked in New York and Chicago; some have been much farther afield—-to Thailand, Hong Kong, New Zealand, and Australia. The result is a dizzying choice of restaurants to suit every mood and situation. You can eat superb French or Italian food, often with an Irish twist; you can have all the fusion you want, with menus that experiment with Asian, Mediterranean, and Californian cuisine; and you'll find plenty of elegant dining rooms, stylish bistros, relaxing hideaways, and late-night eateries to boot.

Irish food is enjoying a renaissance, thanks to talented, imaginative chefs determined to put a fresh spin on traditional ingredients. Organic is the buzzword in Irish cuisine, and you'll find some restaurants specializing in organic and free-range food. Fresh produce is being imaginatively treated, too, giving stalwart Irish ingredients such as potatoes, onions, carrots, and cabbage new life. Seafood, lamb, beef, and pork and bacon still provide the backbone for many signature dishes, but there is also great interest in venison, quail, and other game—both wild and farmed. There are dozens of excellent cheeses—such as St. Tola goat cheese from County Clare or Carrigburne Brie from Wexford—most produced by small artisan cheese makers. If one of these farmhouse varieties appears on a menu, make a point of trying it.

While few restaurants in Dublin have dress requirements, men may feel more comfortable in a jacket and tie at fancier places.

We have included some of the city's best addresses for a hearty pub lunch, a popular dining option among Dubliners.

Prices

Value Added Tax (VAT) will automatically be added to your bill— a 12.5% tax on food and a government excise tax on drinks. Before paying, check to see whether service has been included. If it has been included, you can pay it with a credit card; but if it has not, it's more considerate to the staff to leave the tip in cash (10% to 15%) if paying the main bill by credit card.

A word of warning—you will pay for your dining pleasure here: high overheads and staffing costs have pushed up prices, especially in more upscale places. The good news is that, while Dublin doesn't have Starbucks, there are scores of local cafés serving excellent coffee, often with a good sandwich. Small bakeries are beginning to spring up, borrowing trends from all around the world, offering inexpensive pizzas, focaccia, pitas, tacos, and wraps (taking over for the sandwich as the favorite snack).

It's worthwhile to see if the restaurant of your choice offers an early-bird and/or pre- or post-theater menu, with significantly lower set prices at specific times, often from 6 to 7:30 PM.

CATEGORY	COST*
$$$$	over £25
$$$	£20–£25
$$	£15–£20
$	under £15

*All prices are per person for a first course, a main course, and dessert, including sales tax, excluding wine or tip.

CITY CENTER (SOUTHSIDE)
Contemporary

$$$$ **PEACOCK ALLEY.** Conrad Gallagher ran away from school at 12
★ to be a cook in his native County Donegal. By 18 he was sous-chef at the Plaza in New York, and at 19 *chef de cuisine* at the Waldorf-Astoria's Peacock Alley, whose name he has borrowed. His elegant, modern restaurant has a large, airy 120-seat room with a spectacular view over St. Stephen's Green at one end and a view of the white-tiled open kitchen at the other. Gallagher has a penchant for high food, building up food on the plate and dabbing multicolored oils and garnishes with painterly precision. Strikingly inventive dishes include smoked salmon with basmati rice, pear, preserved ginger, soy sauce, and quesadilla; deep-fried crab cakes with *kataifi* (shredded phyllo pastry); and daube of pot-roasted beef. The excellent service and strong wine list add to the experience, as does the towering presence of Gallagher himself. *Fitzwilliam Hotel, St. Stephens Green, tel. 01/478–7015. Reservations essential. AE, DC, MC, V. Closed Sun.*

$$$ **COOKE'S CAFÉ.** Johnny Cooke's Mediterranean bistro is a cool spot for visiting movie stars. Sit out in summer under an awning and watch the people go by, enjoying elegantly presented dishes on huge white Wedgwood plates. Favorites here include pasta with a rich bubbling Gorgonzola sauce, lobster simply grilled with garlic-herb butter, salad scattered with pieces of tender roast duck, and crab salad with spinach, coriander, mango salsa, and lime dressing. Try not to be in a hurry, because the service, through charming, is slow. Upstairs is the grill bar Rhino Room, also owned by Cooke. 14 S. William St., tel. 01/679–0536. *Reservations essential. AE, DC, MC, V.*

$$$ **LA STAMPA.** One of the most dramatic dining rooms in Dublin, ★ La Stampa has huge gilt mirrors and elaborate candelabra that are gloriously over the top and give a sense of occasion to the simplest meal. The menu changes frequently to reflect an eclectic, international style. For a main course, you may get rack of organic lamb with braised beans, tomatoes, and rosemary jus, roast scallops with artichoke mash and a tomato vinaigrette, or giant prawns served with garlic or mango mayonnaise. Service is brisk but friendly, and there's always a fun atmosphere. 35 Dawson St., tel. 01/677–8611. AE, DC, MC, V. *No lunch weekends.*

Continental

$$$$ **LOCKS.** Claire Douglas's town-house restaurant, overlooking the Grand Canal, offers a genuinely warm welcome. The dining room is comfortable and old-fashioned, with seating on banquettes, starched table linen, and hearty portions served on antique, ironstone plates. Classic starters include Locks's special potato skins—dished up with a fabulous cream, cheese, and bacon sauce—and excellent smoked salmon. For the main course, there's a choice of traditional fish dishes, Irish lamb, and fillet of beef. Although slightly off the beaten path (a 20-minute walk or a short taxi ride southwest of St. Stephen's Green), it's worth the trip. 1 Windsor Terr., Portobello, tel. 01/454–3391. *Reservations essential. AE, DC, MC, V. Closed Sun. No lunch Sat.*

French

$$$$ **PATRICK GUILBAUD.** This fine restaurant combines superb French ★ cooking with impeccable service. The best food here is simple but flawless: juicy prawns wrapped in a light swaddling of phyllo; roast squab stuffed with cabbage and served with a spicy Madeira jus; and the house specialty dish, Challans duck with honey,

lemon, and soy. Follow that if you can with the *assiette au chocolat* (a plate of five different hot and cold chocolate desserts). The walls of the marvelously lofty dining room are hung with paintings from the owners' private collection. *Hotel Merrion, Upper Merrion St., tel. 01/676–4192. Reservations essential. AE, DC, MC, V. Closed Sun.–Mon. and late Dec.–mid-Jan.*

$$$$ **THORNTON'S.** Owner Kevin Thornton is one of the very best
★ chefs in Ireland, and if you are passionate about food, then this place is a must. The upstairs dining room is simply decorated, creating few distractions from the exquisite cuisine. Thornton's cooking style is light, and his dishes are small masterpieces of structural engineering. In season, he marinates legs of partridge, then debones and reforms the bird, with the breasts presented as a crown. Desserts range from fig ice cream to chocolate mousse. The enormous selection of cheeses is shipped in weekly from the Rungis market in Paris. *1 Portobello Rd., tel. 01/454–9067. Reservations essential. AE, DC, MC, V. Closed Sun.–Mon. No lunch.*

Indian

$$ **KHYBER TANDOORI.** Just a short walk from St. Stephen's Green is this gem of a tandoori restaurant. Although it specializes in Pakistani cuisine, it serves a broad range of Indian dishes. Try the shami kebabs—dainty, spiced patties of minced lamb and lentils— or *kabuli chicken tikka shashlik*, marinated, diced chicken with onions and red and green peppers, which comes bright red and sizzling on an iron platter. Settle in and admire the richly embroidered wall hangings and the great gusts of steam coming from the tandoori oven in the glassed-in area. *44 S. William St., tel. 01/670–4855. AE, DC, MC, V.*

Irish

$$$$ **THE COMMONS RESTAURANT.** This large, elegant dining room is in the basement of historic Newman House (☞ The Center City: Around Trinity College, *in* Here and There). The patio doors open

dublin dining

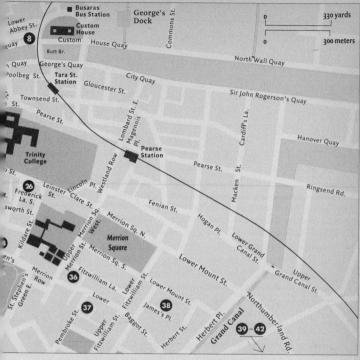

Busaras Bus Station

Custom House

George's Dock

Commons St.

Lower Abbey St.

8

Custom House Quay

Butt Br.

North Wall Quay

Quay

George's Quay

City Quay

Poolbeg St.

Tara St. Station

Gloucester St.

Sir John Rogerson's Quay

Townsend St.

St.

Pearse St.

Lombard St. E.

Magennis Pl.

Cardiff's La.

Hanover Quay

Trinity College

Pearse Station

Westland Row

Pearse St.

Macken St.

Ringsend Rd.

26

Frederick La. S.

Leinster St.

Lincoln Pl.

Clare St.

Fenian St.

Hogan Pl.

Lower Grand Canal St.

sworth St.

Kildare St.

Upper Merrion St.

Merrion Sq. West.

Merrion Sq. N.

Merrion Square

Merrion St.

Merrion Sq. S.

Lower Mount St.

Upper Grand Canal St.

en's

Merrion Row

36

Fitzwilliam La.

Lower Fitzwilliam St.

Lower Mount St.

St. Stephen's Green E.

37

Lower Pembroke St.

Fitzwilliam St.

James's Pl.

38

Herbert Pl.

Northumberland Rd.

Upper Fitzwilliam St.

Baggot St.

Herbert St.

Grand Canal

39 — 42

0 ——— 330 yards

0 ——— 300 meters

O'Connells, **40**
Old Dublin, **13**
Osteria
Romano, **11**
Pasta Fresca, **21**
Patrick
Guilbaud, **36**
Peacock Alley, **19**
The Steps
of Rome, **23**

The Tea
Room, **4**
Thornton's, **32**
Yamamori, **16**

Pub Food
Davy Byrne, **27**
Old Stand, **29**
O'Neill's, **34**
Stag's Head, **35**
Zanzibar, **43**

onto a paved courtyard for summer aperitifs and alfresco lunches. Typical dishes include Irish lamb baked in thyme and black pepper pastry, and loin of rabbit with prawns from Dublin Bay. If you have time, take a stroll in the Iveagh Gardens, an enclosed park that is one of Dublin's best-kept secrets. *85–86 St. Stephen's Green, tel. 01/478–0530. Reservations essential. AE, DC, MC, V. Closed Sat.–Sun.*

$$$ BROWNES BRASSERIE. In a Georgian town house on St. Stephen's Green, now converted to a luxury hotel, is this lovely spot for an intimate lunch or dinner. Huge mirrors reflect the light from crystal chandeliers, glowing on jewel-color walls and upholstery. The food is rich and heartwarming, with classics like Irish smoked salmon, served on warm blini with cream, and confit of duck with lentils. Treat yourself to the lemon tart for dessert. *Brownes Townhouse, 22 St. Stephen's Green, tel. 01/638–3939. Reservations essential. AE, DC, MC, V. No lunch Sat.*

$$–$$$ DOBBINS. Don't be deceived by the sawdust on the floor and the simple decor. It's popular with businesspeople who like the combination of cozy booth seating, friendly service, and classic bistro food. Owner John O'Byrne presides over an impressive cellar with hundreds of wines from around the world. Goat cheese salad and scallops or crab claws drenched in butter are popular starters, while boned brace of quail, with black pudding and foie gras stuffing, is a typical entrée. Lunch can stretch into dinner, which can last well into the night. There is valet parking and the staff are expert at summoning taxis. *15 Stephens La., off Mount St., tel. 01/676–4679. Reservations essential. AE, DC, MC, V. Sun.–Mon.*

$$–$$$ THE LORD EDWARD. Creaking floorboards and an old fireplace give the impression of being in someone's drawing room at this establishment, one of the oldest in the city. Start with traditional fish dishes such as prawn cocktail or smoked salmon, followed by simply cooked Dover sole, salmon, or lobster. Vegetables and potatoes are almost incidental to the fish, but the French fries are excellent, and there's fresh brown bread throughout the meal.

The restaurant is named after Irish revolutionary Lord Edward Fitzgerald, whose remains are buried in St. Werburgh's Church across the road. *23 Christ Church Pl., tel. 01/454–2420. Reservations essential. AE, DC, MC, V. Closed Sun.*

$ BURDOCK'S. Right next door to the Lord Edward is Dublin's famous take-out fish-and-chips shop. Join the inevitable queue and eat in the gardens of St. Patrick's Cathedral, a five-minute walk away. *21 Werburgh St., tel. 01/454–0306. No credit cards.*

$ KILKENNY KITCHEN. On the upper floor of the Kilkenny Shop (☞ Shopping), this big self-service restaurant is an ideal place to take a break from shopping and sightseeing. Homemade soup, casseroles, cold meats, and salads are arranged on a long buffet, along with lots of tasty breads and cakes. Try to get a table by the window overlooking the playing fields of Trinity College. Lunchtime is busy, but it's very pleasant for morning coffee or afternoon tea. *6 Nassau St., tel. 01/677–7066. AE, DC, MC, V.*

Italian

$$ MILANO. The big open kitchen at this bright, cheerful place turns out a wide array of tasty, flashy pizzas, with combinations like tomato and mozzarella, ham and eggs, Cajun with prawns and Tabasco, spinach and egg, or ham and anchovies. There are also simple salads, like tomato and mozzarella with dough balls, and a couple of baked pasta dishes. This is a good place to dine late, with last orders at midnight. Two branches have recently opened up, one in Temple Bar and another on Bachelors Walk along the Quays. *38 Dawson St., tel. 01/670–7744; 18 Essex St. E, Temple Bar, tel. 01/670–3384; 38/39 Lower Ormond Quay, tel. 01/872–0003. AE, MC, V.*

$–$$ IL PRIMO. Old wooden tables and chairs give it a casual feel, and the friendly, if cramped, atmosphere attracts a devoted clientele. The Irish-Italian cuisine is imaginative and reassuring at the same time. Among the main courses, a delicious creamy risotto with chunky chicken breasts, a scattering of chicken livers, and wild mushrooms is a standout. Wine is a specialty. *Montague St., off Harcourt St., tel. 01/478–3373. AE, DC, MC, V. Closed Sun.*

$–$$ PASTA FRESCA. This stylish little Italian restaurant and deli off Grafton Street squeezes a surprising number of people into a fairly small space. Antipasto *misto* (assorted sliced Italian meats) makes a good appetizer—or go for carpaccio *della casa* (wafer-thin slices of beef fillet, with fresh Parmesan, olive oil, lemon juice, and black pepper). The main courses consist of Pasta Fresca's own very good versions of well-known dishes such as spaghetti *alla Bolognese,* cannelloni, and lasagna *al forno.* The pasta is freshly made each day. You'll find lines at lunchtime. *3–4 Chatham St., tel. 01/679–2402. AE, DC, MC, V. Closed Sun.*

$–$$ THE STEPS OF ROME. Just a few steps from Grafton Street, it's perfect for a late-night bite or quick lunch. Slices of homemade pizza can be eaten on the spot or wrapped for takeout. The handful of tables is usually full, but it's worth waiting for classic Italian pasta dishes like pasta parmigiano or pesto, and good fresh salads with focaccia. Follow with zabaglione or tiramisu and good strong espresso. *1 Chatham Ct., tel. 01/670–5630. No credit cards.*

Japanese

$ YAMAMORI. Ramen noodle bars offer a staple diet for budget travelers to Japan, but this is the first in Ireland. The meals-in-a-bowl are a splendid slurping experience, and although you will be supplied with a small Chinese-style soup spoon, the best approach is with chopsticks. You can also get an authentic spin on sushi and sashimi dishes, as well as delicious chicken teriyaki. *71 S. Great George's St., tel. 01/475–5001. AE, DC, MC, V.*

Pan-Asian

$$$ DIEP LE SHAKER. Slightly off the beaten track, on a narrow lane off Pembroke Street, this big, flamboyant restaurant serving

Chinese and Thai food opened in 1999 and was an instant success. Comfortable high-back chairs, pristine table linen, and elegant stemware make this a lovely place to dine—and that's before you experience the superb food. Try the steamed scallops and ginger, or Dover sole served off the bone and encased in a light batter. Don't be surprised to see people ordering champagne to go with their meal. There's a permanent party feel that attracts Ireland's new wealthy set in droves. 55 *Pembroke La., tel. 01/661–1829. AE, DC, MC, V. Closed Sun.*

$$ MAO. Everything is Asian fusion at this bustling café, from the little Andy Warhol pastiche of Chairman Mao on the washroom door to the Ho Fun noodles, stir-fried with shaved beef sirloin, pak choy, garlic, and black beans. It pays homage to Thai, Vietnamese, and other Southeast Asian cuisines. Red snapper is served with a tempura batter, chili mussels come in a large bowl with lemongrass, and vegetarian rice-paper rolls arrive stuffed with shiitake mushrooms and bean-thread noodles. Reservations aren't accepted, so go early to be sure of a seat. 2 *Chatham Row, tel. 01/670–4899. MC, V.*

Russian and Scandinavian

$$$ OLD DUBLIN. Unlikely as it might seem, this brasserie-style restaurant near St. Patrick's Cathedral specializes in Russian and Scandinavian food. A series of cozy but elegant low-ceilinged rooms are decorated with pristine white linens and candlelit tables and warmed by glowing fires in the evening. Familiar dishes such as blini, borscht, chicken Kiev, and beef Stroganoff feature alongside good Irish staples such as roast lamb and fresh baked salmon. The lunch menu tends to be more conventional, while the evening menu has surprises like planked sirloin Hussar, a steak baked between two oak planks, served on an oak platter with salad and sweet pickle. After your meal explore the antiques shops on Francis Street. 90–91 *St. Francis St., tel. 01/454–2028. AE, DC, MC, V. Closed Sun. No lunch Sat.*

Vegetarian

$ NUDE. This place is such a good idea that owner Norman Hewson—brother of U2's Bono—will probably open a chain. A sleek fast-food café, though not fully vegetarian, it serves organic and free-range foods. There are homemade soups, like roasted Italian vegetable or mushroom, and you can get vegetable wraps as well as smoothies and freshly squeezed juices. 21 Suffolk St., tel. 01/672–5577. MC, V.

TEMPLE BAR
American/Casual

$$ ELEPHANT & CASTLE. One of Temple Bar's most popular and established eateries, Elephant & Castle serves up traditional American food—charcoal-grilled burgers, salads, omelets, sandwiches, and pasta. The brunch on Sunday is always packed. The crowds and absence of soft surfaces mean the noise level can be high. When the service is good, the turnover tends to be quick, although you may be inclined to linger, as its formula—an atmosphere that's both bustling and relaxed, generous portions of unfussy and well-prepared food—makes it a casual Dublin standout. New Yorkers take note: yes, this is a cousin of the restaurant of the same name in Greenwich Village. 18 Temple Bar, tel. 01/679–3121. Reservations not accepted. AE, DC, MC, V.

$–$$ BELGO. Part of a Belgium chain of restaurants, it's the perfect place to go if you want a large serving of comfort food and are prepared to be adventurous with what you drink. The menu has dozens of different beers, and the French fries, served alongside omelets, burgers, saucissons (large, flavored Belgian sausages), and steaks, are the best you'll eat in Temple Bar. Go early in the evening (between 5:30 and 7:30) and your bill will match the time you arrived: if you sit down at 6:30 PM you pay £6.30. 17–20 Sycamore St., tel. 01/672–7554. AE, DC, MC, V.

$ BAD ASS CAFÉ. Sinéad O'Connor used to wait tables at this lively spot in a converted warehouse between the Central Bank and Ha'penny Bridge (a "Rock 'n Stroll" tour plaque notes O'Connor's past here). Old-fashioned cash shuttles whiz around the ceiling of the barnlike space, which has bare floors and is painted in primary colors inside and out. A wall of glass makes for great people-watching. Although the food—mostly pizzas and burgers—is unexceptional, the Bad Ass can be a lot of fun and is popular with appetites of all ages. *9–11 Crown Alley, tel. 01/671–2596. AE, MC, V.*

Contemporary

$$$–$$$$ THE TEA ROOM. This restaurant is a good place to go if you have something to celebrate, or if you're hoping to spot some celebrities: it is part of the Clarence hotel (☞ Where To Stay), where stars of stage and screen stay when they're in town. The bright, lofty dining room has spectacular flower arrangements and elegant, modern table settings. The food is adventurous and consistently good, although the menu is not extensive. Try a smoked duck salad or a spectacular baked cheese soufflé, and hope that risotto is on the menu because it always arrives perfectly cooked and superbly flavored. Mouthwatering entrées may include roast scallops, served with new potatoes and seasonal leaves, or grilled corn-fed chicken with goat cheese, pancetta, roast beetroot, and red onion. *Clarence hotel, 6–8 Wellington Quay, tel. 01/670–7766. Reservations essential. AE, MC, V.*

$$$ ★ EDEN. The young owners of several of Dublin's café-style bars, including the Front Lounge and the Globe (☞ Nightlife and the Arts), have followed those successes with a popular brasserie-style restaurant with an open kitchen and high wall of glass looking out onto one of Temple Bar's main squares. Patio-style doors lead to an outdoor eating area—a major plus in a city with relatively few alfresco dining spots. Chef Eleanor Walsh creates such dishes as duck leg confit with lentils and braised hock of ham served with mustard crust and *champ* (creamy, buttery mashed potatoes with scallions). Desserts include rhubarb crème brûlée and homemade ice creams and sorbets. *Meeting House Sq., tel. 01/670–5372. Reservations essential.* AE, MC, V.

\$\$–\$\$\$ MERMAID CAFE. One of the chef-owners dabbles in fine art, and a couple of the large canvases on the walls are carried over into painterly bistro cooking. Lunch, ordered from a blackboard of specials, is an exceptional value—piquant crab cakes, hearty seafood casseroles, venison sausage, or vegetables roasted in a clay dish. Good attention to detail and a thoughtful wine list make this modest restaurant with tall windows looking onto busy Dame Street one of the best eateries in Temple Bar. *69 Dame St., tel. 01/670–8236.* MC, V.

French

\$\$\$–\$\$\$\$ LES FRÈRES JACQUES. This restaurant brings a little bit of Paris
★ to Temple Bar: old prints of Paris and Deauville hang on the green-papered walls, and the French waiters, dressed in white Irish linen and black bow ties, exude a Gallic charm without being excessively formal. Expect traditional French cooking that nods to the seasons. Seafood is a major attraction, and lobster, from the tank, is a specialty, typically roasted and flambéed with Irish whiskey. Also recommended is the *magret de canard* (roast breast of duck served with a ginger and grapefruit sauce). A piano player performs Friday and Saturday evenings and the occasional weeknights. *74 Dame St., tel. 01/679–4555. Reservations essential.* AE, DC, MC, V. *Closed Sun. No lunch Sat.*

Italian

\$–\$\$ OSTERIA ROMANO. Members of the Italian community congregate in the evenings at this cheerful eatery, dishing up authentic Roman cuisine. Specialties include *melanzane parmigiani*, a delicious dish of baked eggplant and cheese, while the pasta list has excellent cream-based dishes, like spaghetti alfredo and carbonara. Beware of finishing the meal with too many flaming *sambucas* (anise-flavored, semisweet Italian liqueur). The best table is by the window overlooking the street. *5 Crow St., tel. 01/670–8662. AE, DC, MC, V.*

Mediterranean

$$–$$$ BRUNO'S. Experienced French-born restaurateur Bruno Berta has a hit on his hands with his French-Mediterranean bistro on one of the busiest corners in Temple Bar. Low-slung windows let you watch passersby. Simple but stylish dishes range from starters of fresh crab claws with chilies, lemongrass, and tomato concassé to main dishes of grilled chicken with raisins, dried prunes, Moroccan semolina, and walnut dressing. Friendly service and a relaxed atmosphere make this one of the best bets in the area. *30 Essex St. E, tel. 01/670–6767. AE, DC, MC, V. Closed Sun.*

SOUTH CITY CENTER: BALLSBRIDGE, DONNYBROOK, AND STILLORGAN
Contemporary

$$–$$$ O'CONNELLS. This recently opened restaurant puts an emphasis on fresh Irish produce and baked goods. The dining room is a vast, modern space with sleek timber paneling and floor-to-ceiling windows. Go for the spit-roasted chicken, or anything baked in the huge clay oven that came all the way from Australia. Other tasty dishes are warm salad of kidneys with greens and oyster mushrooms, or monkfish with a lively pepper, tomato, and coriander salsa. The wine list gives interesting notes on each of the reasonably priced French and New World wines. A huge array of fresh breads is on display in the open kitchen, which turns into a buffet for breakfast and lunch. *Merrion Rd., Ballsbridge, tel. 01/647–3400. AE, DC, MC, V.*

Continental

$$$$ LE COQ HARDI. For many years John Howard has been running
★ one of Dublin's best restaurants. Meeting the challenge posed

by newer restaurants and younger chefs, he continues to refine and reinvent his own cooking. One of Howard's signature dishes— a little old-fashioned, perhaps, but still popular—is Coq Hardi, chicken stuffed with potatoes and mushrooms, wrapped in bacon before going into the oven, and finished off with a dash of Irish whiskey. The cheese boards are among the best in the country, and desserts tend to be rich and sumptuously classical French. Service is friendly and relaxed in the plush, comfortable, and quietly elegant dining room. The wine cellar holds many of the world's great wines. *35 Pembroke Rd., Ballsbridge, tel. 01/668–9070. Reservations essential. AE, DC, MC, V. Closed Sun.*

$$$ BEAUFIELD MEWS. A 10-minute taxi ride from the city center, this 18th-century coach house with stables still has its original cobbled courtyard and is even said to be haunted by a friendly monk. Inside it's all black beams, old furniture, and bric-a-brac. The more desirable tables overlook the courtyard or the garden or are, less predictably, "under the nun" (the nun in question is a 17th-century portrait). While the main attraction is the atmosphere, the food is based on fresh ingredients, and you'll find old favorites like roast duckling à l'orange as well as wild-salmon steaks simply grilled. *Woodlands Ave., Stillorgan, tel. 01/288–0375. Reservations essential. AE, DC, V. Closed Mon.*

Irish

$$$ ERNIE'S RESTAURANT. High-quality ingredients, attention to detail, and consistency are the hallmarks of this long-established restaurant only a few minutes by taxi from the city center. Built around a large tree and fountain, the place has a welcoming atmosphere; it's also well known for the late Ernie Evans's large collection of paintings of the West of Ireland. Blue Irish linen and sparkling crystal decorate tables. The seasonal menu always has a variety of catches of the day—grilled sole with spring onion and thyme butter and poached wild salmon on a bed of creamed potato—as well as four or five meat and poultry entrées such as roasted rack of Wicklow lamb with a caramelized onion tart. *Mulberry Gardens, Donnybrook, tel. 01/269–3300. AE, DC, MC, V. Closed Sun.–Mon. and 1 wk at Christmas. No lunch Sat.*

CITY CENTER (NORTHSIDE)
Contemporary

$$$$ **THE HALO.** This restaurant in the chic Morrison hotel (☞ Where to Stay) has been an instant hit with the fashion crowd and lawyers from the nearby Four Courts. The dramatic dining room with a soaring ceiling and minimalist decor, devised by fashion designer John Rocha, looks moody and mysterious by night, a little forbidding by day. The emphasis here is on complex dishes that look as good as they taste: salmon with a divine hollondaise sauce, served in a Chinese spoon resting on a black platter; fish and vegetable tempura; and chicken stuffed with fresh greens, served with shiitake mushrooms and black bean sauce, are among the specialties. Desserts are miniature works of art on enormous China platters. *Morrison hotel, Ormond Quay, tel. 01/887–2421. AE, DC, MC, V.*

$$–$$$ **CHAPTER ONE.** In the vaulted, stone-walled basement of the Dublin Writers Museum, just down the street from the Hugh Lane Municipal Gallery of Modern Art (☞ North of the Liffey in Here and There), this is one of the most notable restaurants in northside Dublin. Try the pressed duck and black pudding terrine with pear chutney as well as the roast scallops with smoked bacon and potato-herb salad in a chili dressing. The rich bread-and-butter pudding and the apple and pecan crumble are two stellar desserts. *18–19 Parnell Sq., tel. 01/873–2266. Reservations essential. AE, DC, MC, V. Closed Sun.–Mon. No lunch Sat.*

$$ **HARBOUR MASTER.** The main attraction of this big, airy restaurant and bar in the Irish Financial Services Centre north of the Liffey is its setting overlooking a canal basin. At lunch the place is packed with stockbrokers and lawyers; dinner is more subdued.

There's a cavernous bar where you can dine bistro style, but head for the newly built section, which serves hearty food such as seafood risotto, braised lamb shank with lentils and mash, and rib-eye steak with chips. *Custom House Docks, tel. 01/670–1688. AE, DC, MC, V.*

PUB FOOD

Most pubs serve food at lunchtime, some throughout the day. Food ranges from hearty soups and stews to chicken curries, smoked-salmon salads, and sandwiches, and much of it is surprisingly good. Expect to pay £4–£6 for a main course. Some of the larger, more popular pubs may take credit cards.

DAVY BYRNE'S. James Joyce immortalized Davy Byrne's in his sprawling novel *Ulysses*. Nowadays it's more akin to a cocktail bar than a Dublin pub, but it's good for fresh and smoked salmon, salads, and a hot daily special. *21 Duke St., tel. 01/671–1298.*

OLD STAND. Conveniently close to Grafton Street, the Old Stand serves grilled food, including steaks. *37 Exchequer St., tel. 01/677–7220.*

O'NEILL'S. This fine pub, a stone's throw from Trinity College, has the best carvery (open from noon to 2:30) of any pub in the city, serving up a hearty lunch for about £5–£6. *2 Suffolk St., tel. 01/679–3614.*

STAG'S HEAD. With one of Dublin's best pub lunches, the Stag's Head is a favorite of both Trinity students and businesspeople. *1 Dame Ct., tel. 01/679–3701.*

ZANZIBAR. This spectacular and immense bar on the northside of the Liffey looks as though it might be more at home in downtown Marakesh. While away an afternoon on one of its many wicker chairs and enjoy freshly made sandwiches, salads, and cocktails. *34–35 Lower Ormond Quay, tel. 01/878–7212.*

Eating Well is the Best Revenge

Eating out is a major part of every travel experience. It's a chance to explore flavors you don't find at home. And often the walking you do on vacation means that you can dig in without guilt.

START AT THE TOP By all means take in a really good restaurant or two while you're on the road. A trip is a time to kick back and savor the pleasures of the palate. Read up on the culinary scene before you leave home. Check out representative menus on the Web—some chefs have gone electronic. And ask friends who have just come back. Then reserve a table as far in advance as you can, remembering that the best establishments book up months in advance. Remember that some good restaurants require you to reconfirm the day before or the day of your meal. Then again, some really good places will call you, so make sure to leave a number where you can be reached.

ADVENTURES IN EATING A trip is the perfect opportunity to try food you can't get at home. So leave yourself open to try an ethnic food that's not represented where you live or to eat fruits and vegetables you've never heard of. One of them may become your next favorite food.

BEYOND GUIDEBOOKS You can rely on the restaurants you find in these pages. But also look for restaurants on your own. When you're ready for lunch, ask people you meet where they eat. Look for tiny holes-in-the-wall with a loyal following and the best burgers or crispiest pizza crust. Find out about local chains whose fame rests upon a single memorable dish. There's hardly a food-lover who doesn't relish the chance to share a favorite place. It's fun to come up with your own special find—and asking about food is a great way to start a conversation.

SAMPLE LOCAL FLAVORS Do check out the specialties. Is there a special brand of ice cream or a special dish that you simply must try?

HAVE A PICNIC Every so often eat al fresco. Grocery shopping gives you a whole different view of a place.

In This Chapter

Updated by Anto Howard

shopping

IN DAYS GONE BY, travelers would arrive in Ireland, land of leprechauns, shillelaghs, and shamrocks, and quickly realize that the only known specimens of leprechauns or shillelaghs were those in souvenir-shop windows, while shamrocks mainly bloomed around the borders of Irish linen handkerchiefs and tablecloths. All of this is still true, of course, but today you'll find so much more. The variety and sophistication of stores in Dublin now are quite remarkable, as a walk through Dublin's central shopping area, from O'Connell to Grafton Street, proves. Department stores stocking internationally known fashion-designer goods and housewares stand beside small boutiques that make shopping in the city a personalized and pleasurable experience. Prices can be higher in the smaller shops, but the department stores are less likely to stock specifically Irish crafts.

Shopping in central Dublin can mean pushing through crowds, especially in the afternoons and on weekends. Most large shops and department stores are open Monday–Saturday 9–6. Although nearly all department stores are closed on Sunday, some smaller specialty shops stay open. Those with later closing hours are noted below. You're particularly likely to find sales in January, February, July, and August. Don't get confused by the two prices quoted on all goods. As of January 1, 1999, all items had to be listed in euros as well as Irish pounds.

SHOPPING STREETS

Dublin's dozen or so main shopping streets each have a different character, and it's only by visiting them all that you can really appreciate just how wide a range of items are for sale here. The main commercial streets north of the river have chain stores and lackluster department stores that tend to be less expensive and less design-conscious than their counterparts in the city center on the other side of the Liffey.

City Center (Northside)

HENRY STREET. Running westward from O'Connell Street, this is the spot where middle-class Dublin shops. Arnotts department store is the anchor; a host of smaller, specialty stores sell CDs, footwear, and fashion. Henry Street's continuation, Mary Street, has a branch of Marks & Spencer and the Jervis Shopping Centre (☞ *below*).

O'CONNELL STREET. One of Dublin's largest department stores, Clery's, faces the GPO across the city's main thoroughfare—more downscale than southside city streets but still worth a walk. On the same side of the street as the post office is Eason's, a large book, magazine, and stationery store.

City Center (Southside)

DAWSON STREET. Just east of Grafton Street between Nassau Street to the north and St. Stephen's Green to the south, this is the city's primary bookstore avenue, with Waterstone's and Hodges Figgis facing each other on different sides of the street (☞ Books, *below*).

GRAFTON STREET. Dublin's bustling pedestrian-only main shopping street has two upscale department stores, Marks & Spencer and Brown Thomas. The rest of the street is taken up by smaller shops, many of them branches of international chains such as the Body Shop and Bally, and many British chains. This is also

Paris, France.

Paris, Texas.

When it Comes to Getting Local Currency at an ATM, Same Thing.

Whether you're in Yosemite or Yemen, using your Visa card or ATM card with the PLUS symbol is the easiest and most convenient way to get local currency. For example, let's say you're in France. When you make a withdrawal, using your secured PIN, it's dispensed in francs, but is debited from your account in U.S. dollars. This makes it easy to take advantage of favorable exchange rates. And if you need help finding one of Visa's 627,000 ATMs in 127 countries worldwide, visit **visa.com/pd/atm**. We'll make finding an ATM as easy as finding the Eiffel Tower, the Pyramids or even the Grand Canyon.

It's Everywhere You Want To Be.

SEE THE WORLD
IN FULL COLOR

Fodor's Exploring Guides bring all the great sights vividly to life with hundreds of photographs, fascinating historical background, and colorful anecdotes. Detailed maps and practical information keep you headed in the right direction.

Pair a Fodor's Exploring Guide with your trusted Fodor's Pocket Guide for a complete planning package.

Fodor's EXPLORING GUIDES

At bookstores everywhere.

the spot to buy fresh flowers, available at reasonable prices from a number of outdoor stands. Smaller streets off Grafton Street, especially Duke Street, South Anne Street, and Chatham Street, have worthwhile crafts, clothing, and designer housewares shops.

FRANCIS STREET. The Liberties, the oldest part of the city, is the hub of Dublin's antiques trade. This street and surrounding areas, such as the Coombe, have plenty of shops where you can browse. If you're looking for something in particular, dealers will gladly recommend the appropriate store to you.

NASSAU STREET. Dublin's main tourist-oriented thoroughfare has some of the best-known stores selling Irish goods, but you won't find many locals shopping here. Still, if you're looking for classic Irish gifts to take home, you should be sure at least to browse along here.

TEMPLE BAR. Dublin's hippest neighborhood is dotted with small, precious boutiques—mostly intimate, quirky shops that traffic in a small selection of très trendy goods, from vintage wear to some of the most avant-garde Irish clothing you'll find anywhere in the city.

SHOPPING CENTERS
City Center (Northside)

ILAC CENTER (Henry St.) was Dublin's first large, modern shopping center, with two department stores, hundreds of specialty shops, and several restaurants. The stores are not as exclusive as at some of the other centers, but there's plenty of free parking.

JERVIS SHOPPING CENTRE (Jervis and Mary Sts.), opened in late 1996, is Dublin's newest city-center shopping mall; it brought with it the major British chain stores.

dublin shopping

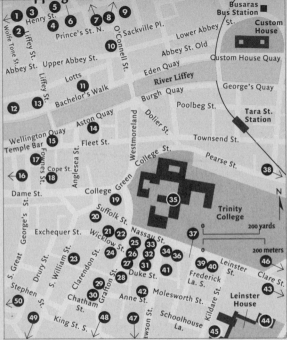

City Center (Southside)

POWERSCOURT TOWNHOUSE CENTRE (59 S. William St.), the former town home of Lord Powerscourt and built in 1771, has an interior courtyard that has been refurbished and roofed over; a pianist often plays on the dais at ground-floor level. Coffee shops and restaurants share space with a mix of antiques and crafts stores, including the **HQ Gallery,** the main showcase of the Irish Craft Council and one of the finest places in Dublin to buy contemporary crafts. You can also buy original Irish fashions here by young designers like Gráinne Walsh.

ROYAL HIBERNIAN WAY (off Dawson St. between S. Anne and Duke Sts.) is on the former site of the two-centuries-old Royal Hibernian Hotel, a coaching inn that was demolished in 1983. The stylish shops are small in scale and include a branch of Leonidas, the Belgian chocolate firm.

ST. STEPHEN'S GREEN CENTRE (northwest corner of St. Stephen's Green), Dublin's largest and most ambitious shopping center, resembles a giant greenhouse, with ironwork in the Victorian style. On three floors overlooked by a vast clock, the 100 mostly small shops sell a variety of crafts, fashions, and household goods.

TOWER DESIGN CENTRE (Pearse St., tel. 01/677–5655), east of the heart of the city center (near the Waterways Visitor Centre), has more than 35 separate crafts shops in a converted 1862 sugar-refinery tower. On the ground floor, you can stop at workshops devoted to heraldry and Irish pewter; the other six floors feature hand-painted silks, ceramics, hand-knit items, jewelry, and fine-art cards and prints.

County Dublin Suburbs

BLACKROCK (Blackrock, Co. Dublin), to the south, is technically outside of Dublin's city center, but it deserves special mention as one of the most customer-friendly shopping centers around. It's built on two levels, looking onto an inner courtyard, with the giant Superquinn Foodstore, cafés, and restaurants. Blackrock can be reached conveniently on the DART train line; it has its own stop.

BLANCHARDSTOWN (Blanchardstown, Dublin 15) is the biggest shopping center in the country. It's a good spot for bargains and a chance to see Dublin families about their everyday lives. The No. 39 bus from Lower Abbey Street goes to Blanchardstown.

DEPARTMENT STORES

ARNOTTS (Henry St., tel. 01/872–1111) has a wide variety of clothing, household, and sporting goods filling three complete floors; the smaller Grafton Street branch (Grafton St., tel. 01/872–1111) stocks only new fashion and footwear.

A-WEAR (Grafton St., tel. 01/671–7200; Henry St., tel. 01/872–4644) is a line of shops specializing in fashion for men and women. Many of the items are seasonal and closely follow the ever-changing styles. A steady stream of clothing is supplied by leading Irish designers, including John Rocha.

BROWN THOMAS (Grafton St., tel. 01/679–5666), Dublin's most exclusive department store, stocks the leading designer names in clothing and cosmetics and a wide variety of stylish accessories. It also carries clothing by Irish designers.

CLERY'S (O'Connell St., tel. 01/878–6000) was once the city's most fashionable department store and is still worth a visit, despite its rapidly aging decor. It has four floors of all types of merchandise—from fashion to home appliances—and caters to a distinctly modest, traditional sense of style.

DUNNES STORES (St. Stephen's Green Centre, tel. 01/478–0188; Henry St., tel. 01/872–6833; Ilac Shopping Center, Mary St., tel. 01/873–0211) is Ireland's largest chain of department stores. All stores stock fashion, household, and grocery items and have a reputation for value and variety.

EASON'S (O'Connell St., tel. 01/873–3811; Ilac Shopping Center, Mary St., tel. 01/872–1322) is known primarily for its wide variety of books, magazines, and stationery; its larger O'Connell Street branch now sells tapes, CDs, records, videos, and other audiovisual goodies.

MARKS & SPENCER (Grafton St., tel. 01/679–7855; Henry St., tel. 01/872–8833), perennial competitor to Brown Thomas (☞ *above*), stocks everything from fashion (including lingerie) to tasty, unusual groceries. The Grafton Street branch even has its own bureau de change, which doesn't charge commission.

OUTDOOR MARKETS

Dublin has a number of open-air markets. **Moore Street,** behind the Ilac center, is open Monday–Saturday 9–6. Stalls lining both sides of the street sell fruits and vegetables; it's also a good spot to come to buy shoes and boots. The traditional Dublin repartee here is renowned in the city. Other open markets are only open on weekends. A variety of bric-a-brac is sold at the **Liberty Market** on the north end of Meath Street, open on Friday and Saturday 10–6, Sunday noon–5:30. The indoor **Mother Redcap's Market,** opposite Christ Church, is open Friday–Sunday 10–5; come here for antiques and bric-a-brac.

SPECIALTY SHOPS
Antiques

Dublin is one of Europe's best cities in which to buy antiques, largely due to a long and proud tradition of restoration and high-quality craftmanship. The Liberties, Dublin's oldest district, is fittingly the hub of the antiques trade and is chock-a-block with shops and traders. Bachelor's Walk, along the quays, also has some decent shops. Although the economic boom has created quite a seller's market, bargains are still possible.

ANTIQUES AND COLLECTIBLES FAIRS (tel. 01/670–8295) take place at Newman House (85–86 St. Stephen's Green) every second Sunday throughout the year.

CONLON ANTIQUES (21 Clanbrassil St., tel. 01/453–7323) has a wide selection of antiques, from sideboards to fanlights.

HA'PENNY BRIDGE GALLERIES (15 Bachelor's Walk, tel. 01/872–3950) has four floors of curios, with a particularly large selection of bronzes, silver, and china.

O'SULLIVAN ANTIQUES (43–44 Francis St., tel. 01/454–1143 or 01/453–9659) specializes in 18th- and 19th-century furniture and has a high-profile clientele, including Mia Farrow and Liam Neeson.

Books

You won't have any difficulty weighing down your suitcase with books: Ireland, after all, produced four Nobel literature laureates in just under 75 years. If you're at all interested in modern and contemporary literature, be sure to leave yourself time to browse through the bookstores, as you're likely to find books available here you can't find back home. Best of all, thanks to an enlightened national social policy, there's no tax on books, so if you only buy books, you don't have to worry about getting VAT slips.

BOOKS UPSTAIRS (36 College Green, tel. 01/679–6687) carries an excellent range of special-interest books, including gay and feminist literature, psychology, and self-help books.

CATHACH BOOKS (10 Duke St., tel. 01/671–8676) sells first editions of Irish literature and many other books of Irish interest, plus old maps of Dublin and Ireland.

DUBLIN BOOKSHOP (24 Grafton St., tel. 01/677–5568) is an esteemed, family-owned bookstore.

FRED HANNA'S (29 Nassau St., tel. 01/677–1255) sells old and new books, with a good choice of works on travel and Ireland.

GREENE'S (Clare St., tel. 01/676–2544) carries an extensive range of secondhand volumes.

HODGES FIGGIS (56–58 Dawson St., tel. 01/677–4754), Dublin's leading independent, stocks 1½ million books on three floors; there's also a pleasant café on the first floor.

HUGHES & HUGHES (St. Stephen's Green Centre, tel. 01/478-3060), has strong travel and Irish interest sections. There is also a store at Dublin Airport.

WATERSTONE'S (7 Dawson St., tel. 01/679–1415), a large branch of the British chain, has two floors featuring a fine selection of Irish and international books.

WINDING STAIR (40 Ormond Quay, Dublin 1, tel. 01/873–3292) is a charming new- and used-book store overlooking the Liffey. The little upstairs café is the perfect spot for an afternoon of reading.

China, Crystal, Ceramics, and Jewelry

Ireland is synonymous with Waterford crystal, which is available in a wide range of products, including relatively inexpensive items. But other lines are now gaining recognition, such as Cavan, Galway, and Tipperary crystal. **Brown Thomas** (☞ *above*) is the best department store for crystal; the best specialty outlets are listed below.

BLARNEY WOOLLEN MILLS (21–23 Nassau St., tel. 01/671–0068) is one of the best places for Belleek china, Waterford and Galway crystal, and Irish linen.

CRAFTS CENTRE OF IRELAND (Stephen's Green Centre, tel. 01/475–4526) has an impressive inventory of Ireland's most famous contemporary designers, including Michael Kennedy and Diane McCormick (ceramics), Glen Lucas (woodturning), and Jerpoint Glass (glassworks).

CRANNÓG (Crown Alley, tel. 01/671–0805), in Temple Bar, specializes in ceramics and contemporary Irish jewelry, especially silver pendants and rings.

DESIGNYARD (E. Essex St., tel. 01/677–8453) carries beautifully designed Irish and international tableware, lighting, small furniture, and jewelry.

HOUSE OF IRELAND (37–38 Nassau St., tel. 01/671–6133) has an extensive selection of crystal, jewelry, tweeds, sweaters, and other upscale goods.

KILKENNY SHOP (5–6 Nassau St., tel. 01/677–7066) specializes in contemporary Irish-made ceramics, pottery, and silver jewelry and also holds regular exhibits of exciting new work by Irish craftspeople.

MCDOWELL (3 Upper O'Connell St., tel. 01/874–4961), a jewelry shop popular with Dubliners, has been in business for more than 100 years.

TIERNEYS (St. Stephen's Green Centre, tel. 01/478–2873) carries a good selection of crystal and china. Claddagh rings, pendants, and brooches are popular buys.

WEIR & SONS (96 Grafton St., tel. 01/677–9678), Dublin's most prestigious jewelers, sells a wide range of goods in addition to jewelry and watches, including china, glass, lamps, silver, and leather.

Museum Stores

NATIONAL GALLERY OF IRELAND SHOP (Merrion Sq. W, tel. 01/678–5450) has a terrific selection of books on Irish art, plus posters, postcards, note cards, and a wide array of lovely bibelots.

NATIONAL MUSEUM SHOP (Kildare St., tel. 01/677–7444 ext. 327) carries jewelry based on ancient Celtic artifacts in the museum collection, contemporary Irish pottery, a large selection of books, and other gift items.

TRINITY COLLEGE LIBRARY SHOP (Old Library, Trinity College, tel. 01/608–2308) sells Irish-theme books, *Book of Kells* souvenirs of all kinds, plus clothing, jewelry, and other lovely Irish-made items.

Music

An increasing amount of Irish-recorded material—including traditional folk music, country-and-western, rock, and even a smattering of classical music—is available.

CELTIC NOTE (12 Nassau St., tel. 01/670–4157), **Claddagh Records** (2 Cecilia St., Temple Bar, tel. 01/679–3664), and **Gael Linn** (26 Merrion Sq., tel. 01/676–7283) specialize in traditional Irish-music and Irish-language recordings.

HMV (65 Grafton St., tel. 01/679–5334; 18 Henry St., tel. 01/872–2095) is one of the larger record shops in town.

MCCULLOGH PIGGOTT (25 Suffolk St., tel. 01/677–3138) is the best place in town for instruments, sheet music, scores, and books about music.

TOWER RECORDS (6–8 Wicklow St., tel. 01/671–3250) is the best-stocked international chain.

VIRGIN MEGASTORE (14–18 Aston Quay, tel. 01/677–7361) is Dublin's biggest music store and holds in-store performances by Irish bands.

Sweaters and Tweeds

If you think Irish woolens are limited to Aran sweaters and tweed jackets, you'll be pleasantly surprised by the range of hats, gloves, scarves, blankets, and other goods you can find. If you're traveling outside of Dublin, you may want to wait to make purchases

Beyond T-Shirts and Key Chains

You can't go wrong with baseball caps, refrigerator magnets, beer mugs, sweatshirts, T-shirts, key chains, and other local logo merchandise. You won't go broke buying these items, either.

BUDGET FOR A MAJOR PURCHASE If souvenirs are all about keeping the memories alive in the long haul, plan ahead to shop for something really special—a work of art, a rug or something else hand-crafted, or a major accessory for your home. One major purchase will stay with you far longer than a dozen tourist trinkets, and you'll have all the wonderful memories associated with shopping for it besides.

ADD TO YOUR COLLECTION Whether antiques, used books, salt and pepper shakers, or ceramic frogs are your thing, start looking in the first day or two. Chances are you'll want to scout around and then go back to some of the first shops you visited before you hand over your credit card.

GET GUARANTEES IN WRITING Is the vendor making promises? Ask him to put them in writing.

ANTICIPATE A SHOPPING SPREE If you think you might buy breakables, include a length of bubble wrap. Pack a large tote bag in your suitcase in case you need extra space. Don't fill your suitcase to bursting before you leave home. Or include some old clothing that you can leave behind to make room for new acquisitions.

KNOW BEFORE YOU GO Study prices at home on items you might consider buying while you're away. Otherwise you won't recognize a bargain when you see one.

PLASTIC, PLEASE Especially if your purchase is pricey and you're looking for authenticity, it's always smart to pay with a credit card. If a problem arises later on and the merchant can't or won't resolve it, the credit-card company may help you out.

elsewhere, but if Dublin is it, you still have plenty of good shops to choose from. The tweed on sale in Dublin comes from two main sources, Donegal and Connemara; labels inside the garments guarantee their authenticity. Following are the largest retailers of traditional Irish woolen goods in the city.

AN TÁIN (13 Temple Bar Sq. N, tel. 01/679–0523) carries hyperstylish handmade Irish sweaters, jackets, and accessories.

BLARNEY WOOLLEN MILLS (21–23 Nassau St., tel. 01/671–0068) has a good selection of tweed, linen, and woolen sweaters in all price ranges.

CLEO LTD. (18 Kildare St., tel. 01/676–1421) sells hand-knit sweaters and accessories made only from natural fibers; it also carries its own designs.

DUBLIN WOOLLEN MILLS (Metal Bridge Corner, tel. 01/677–5014) at Ha'penny Bridge has a good selection of hand-knit and other woolen sweaters at competitive prices.

KEVIN AND HOWLIN (31 Nassau St., tel. 01/677–0257) specializes in handwoven tweed men's jackets, suits, and hats and also sells tweed fabric.

MONAGHAN'S (Grafton Arcade, 15–17 Grafton St., tel. 01/677–0823) specializes in cashmere.

Vintage

FLIP (4 Upper Fownes St., tel. 01/671–4299), one of the original stores in Temple Bar, sells vintage and retro clothing from the '50s, '60s, and '70s.

In This Chapter

Updated by Anto Howard

outdoor activities and sports

HEALTH CLUBS ARE RELATIVELY NEW to the city, but they're starting to flourish (especially at hotels). Yet there are plenty of other ways to get out and move about. You can explore a beach; cheer on a hometown team; or walk, run, horseback-ride, or bike through Phoenix Park.

BEACHES

To the north of Dublin city is **North Bull Island,** created over the years by the action of the tides and offering an almost 3-km-long (2-mi-long) stretch of fine sand. Bus 130 from Lower Abbey Street stops by the walkway to the beach. **Malahide,** a charming village on the northside DART line, has a clean and easily accessible beach, though the current can be strong. The main beach for swimming on the south side of Dublin is at **Killiney** (13 km/8 mi south of the city center), a shingly beach stretching for 3 km (2 mi). The DART train station is right by the beach; the stop is called Killiney. Near Dublin city center, **Sandymount Strand** is a long expanse of fine sand where the tide goes out nearly 3 km (2 mi), but it's not suitable for swimming or bathing because the tide races in so fast. The strand can be reached easily by the DART train.

PARTICIPANT SPORTS

If it's essential that you get in a daily workout, you should be able to do so while you're in Dublin, although it will probably take some careful planning. For all its recent changes, the city has only recently embraced health clubs and fitness centers. Check the service information provided for each hotel (☞ Where To Stay) for particular fitness amenities; if none are listed, call to inquire, as many of the hotels are adding these amenities.

Bicycling

Bicycling is not recommended in the city center, as traffic is heavy and most roads don't have shoulders, much less bike lanes. Phoenix Park and some suburbs (especially Ballsbridge, Clontarf, and Sandymount), however, are pleasant for biking once you're off the main roads. To the immediate south of Dublin, the Dublin and Wicklow mountains provide plenty of challenging terrain. Care should always be taken in securing your bicycle when it's left unattended.

Bicycles can be rented for about £35 a week, with an equivalent amount charged for deposit. Nearly 20 companies in the Dublin region rent bicycles; Tourist Information Offices (TIOs) have a full list. Some of the best include the following: **Joe Daly** (Lower Main St., Dundrum, tel. 01/298–1485); **McDonald's** (38 Wexford St., tel. 01/475–2586); **Mike's Bike Shop** (Dun Laoghaire Shopping Center, tel. 01/280–0417); and **Tracks Cycles** (8 Botanic Rd., Glasnevin, tel. 01/873–2455).

Bowling

Bowling is a popular sport in Dublin; two kinds are played locally. The sedate, outdoor variety is played at **Herbert Park** (Ballsbridge, tel. 01/660–1875) and at **Kenilworth Bowling Club** (Grosvenor Sq., tel. 01/497–2305). The city has six indoor 10-pin bowling centers: **Bray Bowl** (Quinsboro Rd., tel. 01/286–4455); **Leisureplex Coolock** (Malahide Rd., tel. 01/848–5722; Village Green Center, Tallaght, tel. 01/459–9411); **Metro Bowl** (149 N. Strand Rd., tel. 01/855–0400); **Stillorgan Bowl** (Stillorgan, tel. 01/288–1656); and **Superdome** (Palmerstown, tel. 01/626–0700).

Golf

The Dublin region is an idyllic place for golfers, with 30 18-hole courses and 15 9-hole courses, and several more on the way. Major 18-hole courses include the following: **Deer Park** (Howth, tel. 01/832–6039); **Edmonstown** (Rathfarnham, tel. 01/493–2461); **Elm Park** (Donnybrook, tel. 01/269–3438); **Foxrock** (Torquay Rd., tel. 01/289–3992); **Hermitage** (Lucan, tel. 01/626–4781); **Newlands** (Clondalkin, tel. 01/459–2903); **Sutton** (Sutton, tel. 01/832–3013); and **Woodbrook** (Bray, tel. 01/282–4799).

Health Clubs

The health craze has reached laconic Dublin, and health clubs are springing up all over the city. The **Iveagh Fitness Club** (Christ Church St., Dublin 8, tel. 01/454–6555) is right next to Christ Church Cathedral and has a pool, sauna, and full weight room. Just off Grafton Street, the **Jackie Skelly Fitness Centre** (41–42 Clarendon St., Dublin 2 tel. 01/677–0040) is perfect if you're staying in a city-center hotel without a gym.

Horseback Riding

Dublin's environs are excellent for horseback riding. Stables on the city outskirts give immediate access to suitable riding areas. In the city itself, Phoenix Park provides superb, quiet riding conditions away from the busy main road that bisects the park. About 20 riding stables in the greater Dublin area have horses for hire by the hour or the day, for novices and experienced riders; a few also operate as equestrian centers and have lessons. Major stables in the area include the following: **Brittas Lodge Riding Stables** (Brittas, tel. 01/458–2726) and **Deerpark Riding Center** (Castleknock Rd., Castleknock, tel. 01/820–7141). Outside Dublin, Counties Dublin, Kildare, Louth, Meath, and Wicklow all have unspoiled country territory ideal for horseback riding.

Jogging

Traffic in Dublin is heavy from early morning until late into the night and it's getting worse, so if you're used to jogging the streets back home be aware that here you'll have to dodge vehicles and stop for lights. (Remember *always* to look to your right *and* your left before crossing a street.) If you're staying in Temple Bar or on the western end of the city and you can run 9 km (5½ mi), head to Phoenix Park, easily the nicest place in the city for a jog. If you're on the southside, Merrion Square, St. Stephen's Green, and Trinity College are all good places for short jogs, though be prepared to dodge pedestrians; if you're looking for a longer route, ask your hotel to direct you to the Grand Canal, which has a pleasant path you can run along as far east as the Grand Canal Street Bridge.

Swimming

Dublin has 12 public pools; recommended are **Townsend Street** (Townsend St., tel. 01/677–0503) and **Williams Park** (Rathmines, tel. 01/496–1275). Private pools open to the public for a small fee are located at **Dundrum Family Recreation Center** (Meadowbrook, Dundrum, tel. 01/298–4654), **Fitzpatrick Castle Hotel** (Killiney, tel. 01/285–0328), **St. Vincent's** (Navan Rd., tel. 01/838–4906), and **Terenure College** (Templeogue Rd., tel. 01/490–7071). For a hardier dip, there's year-round sea swimming at the **Forty Foot Bathing Pool** in Sandycove.

Tennis

Tennis is one of Dublin's most popular participant sports, and some public parks have excellent tennis facilities open to the public. Among the best are **Bushy Park** (Terenure, tel. 01/490–0320); **Herbert Park** (Ballsbridge, tel. 01/668–4364); and **St. Anne's Park** (Dollymount Strand, tel. 01/833–8898). Several private tennis clubs are open to the public, including **Kilternan Tennis Centre** (Kilternan Golf and Country Club Hotel, Kilternan, tel. 01/295–

3729); **Landsdowne Lawn Tennis Club,** (Londonbridge Rd., Dublin 4, tel. 01/668–0219); and **West Wood Lawn Tennis Club** (Leopardstown Racecourse, Foxrock, Dublin 18, tel. 01/289–2911). For more information, contact **Tennis Ireland** (22 Argyle Sq., Donnybrook, Dublin 4, tel. 01/668–1841).

SPECTATOR SPORTS
Gaelic Games

The traditional games of Ireland, Gaelic football and hurling, attract a huge following, with roaring crowds cheering on their county teams. Games are held at **Croke Park,** the national stadium for Gaelic games, just north of the city center. For details of matches, contact the **Gaelic Athletic Association** (Croke Park, tel. 01/836–3222). A museum dedicated to the history of Gaelic games, with plenty of footage from famous games, has recently opened at Croke Park (£3, May–Sept., daily 9:30–5; Oct.–Apr., Tues.–Sat. 10–5, Sun. 12–5).

Greyhound Racing

As elsewhere in the world, Greyhound racing is a sport in decline in Ireland. But the track can still be one of the best places to see Dubliners at their most passionate, among friends, and full of wicked humor. **Harolds Cross** (Harolds Cross, Dublin 6, tel. 01/497–1081) is dilapidated but serves its purpose. **Shelbourne Park** (Shelbourne Park, Dublin 4, tel. 01/668–3502) is a more stylish place where you can book a table in the restaurant overlooking the track.

Horse Racing

Horse racing—from flat to hurdle to steeplechase—is one of the great sporting loves of the Irish. The sport is closely followed and betting is popular, but the social side of attending racing is also important to Dubliners. The main course in Dublin is **Leopardstown** (tel. 01/289–3607), an ultramodern course on the

Temperature & Liquid Volume Conversion Chart

Temperature: Metric Conversions

To change Centigrade or Celsius (C) to Fahrenheit (F), multiply C by 1.8 and add 32. To change F to C, subtract 32 from F and multiply by .555.

C°	F°	F°	C°
0	-17.8	60	15.5
10	-12.2	70	21.1
20	-6.7	80	26.6
30	-1.1	90	32.2
32	0	98.6	37.0
40	+4.4	100	37.7
50	10.0		

Liquid Volume: Liters/U.S. Gallons

To change liters (L) to U.S. gallons (gal), multiply L by .264. To change U.S. gal to L, multiply gal by 3.79.

L to gal	gal to L
1 = .26	1 = 3.8
2 = .53	2 = 7.6
3 = .79	3 = 11.4
4 = 1.1	4 = 15.2
5 = 1.3	5 = 19.0
6 = 1.6	6 = 22.7
7 = 1.8	7 = 26.5
8 = 2.1	8 = 30.3

southside and home of the Hennessey Gold Cup in February, Ireland's most prestigious steeplechase. In the greater Dublin region, other courses include **Fairyhouse** (Co. Meath, tel. 01/825–6167), which every Easter Monday hosts the Grand National, the most popular steeplechase of the season; the **Curragh** (tel. 045/441205), southwest of Dublin, home of the five Classics, the most important flat races of the season, which are run from May to September; and **Punchestown** (tel. 045/897704) outside Naas, County Kildare, home of the ever-popular Punchestown National Hunt Festival in April.

Rugby

International rugby matches are staged during the winter and spring at the vast **Lansdowne Road Stadium.** Local matches are played every weekend, also in winter and spring. For details, contact the **Irish Rugby Football Union** (62 Lansdowne Rd., tel. 01/668–4601).

Soccer

Although soccer—called football in Europe—is very popular in Ireland (largely due to the euphoria resulting from the national team's successes throughout the late 1980s and early '90s), facilities for watching it are not so ideal; they tend to be small and out of date. **Lansdowne Road,** the vast rugby stadium, is the main center for international matches. For details, contact the **Football Association of Ireland** (80 Merrion Sq. S, tel. 01/676–6864).

In This Chapter

Updated by Anto Howard

nightlife and the arts

LONG BEFORE STEPHEN DAEDALUS'S EXCURSIONS into nighttown (read Joyce's *A Portrait of the Artist as a Young Man*), Dublin was proud of its lively after-hours scene, particularly its thriving pubs. Lately, however, with the advent of Irish rock superstars (think U2, the Cranberries, Sinéad O'Connor, Bob Geldof) and the resurgence of Celtic music (think *Riverdance*, the soundtrack to *Titanic*), the rest of the world seems to have discovered that Dublin is one of the most happening places in the world. Most nights the city's pubs and clubs overflow with young cell phone–toting Dubliners and Europeans who descend on the capital for weekend getaways. The city's 900-plus pubs are its main source of entertainment; many public houses in the city center have live music—from rock to jazz to traditional Irish.

A number of newspapers have informative listings: the *Irish Times* has a daily guide to what's happening in Dublin and in the rest of the country, as well as complete film and theater schedules. The *Evening Herald* lists theaters, cinemas, and pubs with live entertainment. *In Dublin* and the *Big Issue* are weekly guides to all film, theater, and musical events around the city. The *Event Guide*, a weekly free paper that lists music, cinema, theater, art shows, and dance clubs, can be found in pubs and cafés around the city. In peak season, consult the free Bord Fáilte leaflet "Events of the Week."

NIGHTLIFE

Dublin has undergone a major nightlife revolution in the last few years and now, for better or worse, bears more than a passing resemblance to Europe's nightclub mecca, London. The old-fashioned discos, once the only alternative for late-night entertainment, have been replaced by a plethora of internationally known dance clubs where style and swagger rule. The streets of the city center, once hushed after the pubs had closed, are the scene of what appears to be a never-ending party; indeed, you're as likely to find crowds at 2 AM on a Wednesday as you are at the same time on a Saturday. Although the majority of clubs cater to an under-30 crowd of trendy students and young professionals eager to sway to the rhythmic throb of electronic dance music, there are plenty of alternatives, including a number of nightclubs where the dominant sounds range from soul to salsa. And if you're looking for something less strenuous, Dublin doesn't disappoint: there are brasseries, bistros, cafés, and all manner of late-night eateries where you can sit, sip, and chat until 2 AM or later.

A relatively new introduction to Dublin's nightclub scene is the professional promoter who organizes theme "parties" and rents space from nightclub owners, paying them a share of the door receipts as rent.

Another trend has been the "reinventing" of some of the old classic pubs—arguably some of the finest watering holes in the world—as popular spots. Despite the changes, the traditional pub has steadfastly clung to its role as the primary center of Dublin's social life. The city has nearly 1,000 pubs ("licensed tabernacles," writer Flann O'Brien calls them). And while the vision of elderly men enjoying a chin wag over a creamy pint of stout has become something of a rarity, there are still plenty of places where you can enjoy a quiet drink and a chat. Last drinks are called at 11:30 PM in spring and summer, and 11 PM in fall and winter; some city-center pubs even have extended opening hours from Thursday through Saturday and don't serve last drinks until 1:45 AM.

A word of warning: Although most pubs and clubs are extremely safe, the lads can get lively—public drunkenness is very much a part of Dublin's nightlife. While this is for the most part seen as the Irish form of unwinding after a long week (or day!), it can sometimes lead to regrettable incidents such as fighting. In an effort to keep potential trouble at bay, bouncers and security men maintain a visible presence in all clubs and many pubs around the city. At the end of the night, the city center is full of young people trying to get home, which makes for extremely long lines at taxi stands and light-night bus stops, especially on weekends. The combination of drunkenness and impatience can sometimes lead to trouble, so act cautiously. If you need late-night transportation, try to arrange it with your hotel before you go out.

Pubs

SOUTH CITY CENTER

BYRNES (Galloping Green, Stillorgan, tel. 01/288–7683) has the airy atmosphere of an old-fashioned country pub, even though it's only 8 km (5 mi) from the city center. It's one of the few pubs that haven't been renovated.

DUBLINER PUB (Jurys Hotel, Ballsbridge, tel. 01/660–5000) has been remade as an old-fashioned Irish pub; it's a busy meeting place at lunch and after work.

JOHN FALLONS (129 Dean St.), a classy public house in the Liberties, has one of the finest snugs in the city and great photos of old Dublin.

KIELY'S (Donnybrook Rd., tel. 01/283–0208), at first glance, appears to be just another modernized pub, but go up the side lane, and you'll find a second pub, Ciss Madden's, in the same building. Even though it was built in 1992, it's an absolutely authentic and convincing reconstruction of an ancient Irish tavern, right down to the glass globe lights and old advertising signs.

KITTY O'SHEA'S (Upper Grand Canal St., tel. 01/660–9965) has Pre-Raphaelite–style stained glass, complementing its lively, sports-oriented atmosphere. Its sister pubs are in Brussels and Paris; this is the original.

O'BRIEN'S (Sussex Terr., tel. 01/668–2594), beside the Doyle Burlington hotel, is a little antique gem of a pub, scarcely changed in 50 years, with traditional snugs.

CITY CENTER

BRAZEN HEAD (Bridge St., tel. 01/677–9549), Dublin's oldest pub (the site has been licensed since 1198), has stone walls and open fires that have changed little over the years. It's renowned for traditional-music performances and for lively sing-along sessions on Sunday evenings. A little difficult to find, the Brazen Head is located on the south side of the Liffey quays; turn down Lower Bridge Street, and then make a right into the old lane.

CAFÉ-EN-SEINE (40 Dawson St., tel. 01/677–4369) is a Parisian-style "locale," with a wrought-iron balcony, art deco furniture, a vaulted ceiling, and a clientele to match: most are young, cell phone–carrying professionals. Café au lait and alcoholic drinks are served all day until closing.

CASSIDY'S (42 Lower Camden St., tel. 01/475–1429) is a quiet neighborhood pub with a pint of stout so good that President Bill Clinton dropped in for one during a visit to Dublin.

CHIEF O'NEILL'S (Smithfield Village, tel. 01/817–3838), Dublin's newest hotel, has a large bar-café with an open, airy atmosphere and often hosts traditional Irish sessions.

The **COBBLESTONE** (N. King St., tel. 01/872–1799) is a glorious house of ale in the best Dublin tradition. Popular with Smithfield market workers, its chatty atmosphere and live music are attracting a wider crowd.

DAVY BYRNE'S (21 Duke St., tel. 01/671–1298) is a pilgrimage stop for Joyceans. In *Ulysses*, Leopold Bloom stops in here for a glass of burgundy and a Gorgonzola cheese sandwich. He then leaves the pub and walks to Dawson Street, where he helps a blind man cross the road. Unfortunately, the much-altered pub is unrecognizable from Joyce's day, but it still serves some fine pub grub.

DOCKERS (5 Sir John Rogerson's Quay, tel. 01/677–1692) is a trendy quayside spot east of city center, just around the corner from Windmill Lane Studios, where U2 and other noted bands record; at night the area is a little dicey, so come during the day.

DOHENY & NESBITT (5 Lower Baggot St., tel. 01/676–2945), a traditional spot with snugs, dark wooden decor, and smoke-darkened ceilings, has hardly changed over the decades.

DOYLE'S (9 College St., tel. 01/671–0616), a small, cozy pub, is a favorite with journalists from the Irish Times, just across the street.

The **GLOBE** (11 S. Great George's St., tel. 01/671–1220), one of the hippest café-bars in town, draws arty, trendy Dubliners who sip espresso drinks by day and pack the place at night. There's live jazz on Sunday.

GROGANS (15 S. William St., tel. 01/677–9320), also known as the Castle Lounge, is a small place packed with creative folk.

GUBU (Capel St., tel. 01/874–0710) is the newest venture north of the river by the hugely successful owners of the Globe (☞ above). The pool table downstairs is a bonus.

HOGAN'S (35 Great St. Georges St., tel. 01/6677–5904), a huge floor space on two levels, is jammed on most nights, but the old place maintains its style through it all and the beer is top class.

HORSESHOE BAR (Shelbourne Méridien Hotel, 27 St. Stephen's Green, tel. 01/676–6471) is a popular meeting place for Dublin's businesspeople and politicians, though it has comparatively little space for drinkers around the semicircular bar.

KEHOE'S (9 S. Anne St., tel. 01/677–8312) is popular with Trinity students and academics. The tiny back room is cozy.

dublin pubs

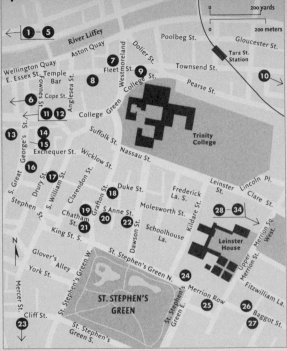

MCDAID'S (3 Harry St., tel. 01/679–4395) attracted boisterous Brendan Behan and other leading writers in the 1950s; its wild literary reputation still lingers, although the bar has been discreetly modernized and the atmosphere is altogether quieter.

MOTHER REDCAP'S TAVERN (Back La., tel. 01/453–8306) is an authentic re-creation of a 17th-century Dublin tavern, with stone walls from an old flour mill, beams, and old prints of the city.

NEARY'S (1 Chatham St., tel. 01/677–7371), which has an exotic Victorian-style interior, was once the haunt of music-hall artists, as well as of a certain literary set including Brendan Behan. Join the actors from the adjacent Gaiety Theatre for a good pub lunch.

O'DONOGHUE'S (15 Merrion Row, tel. 01/676–2807), a cheerful, smoky hangout, has impromptu musical performances that often spill out onto the street.

RYAN'S PUB (28 Parkgate St., tel. 01/677–6097) is one of Dublin's last genuine, late-Victorian-era pubs and has changed little since its last (1896) remodeling.

STAG'S HEAD (1 Dame Ct., tel. 01/679–3701) dates from 1770 and was rebuilt in 1895; theater people from the nearby Olympia, journalists, and Trinity students turn up around the unusual counter, fashioned from Connemara red marble.

TONER'S (139 Lower Baggot St., tel. 01/676–3090), though billed as a Victorian bar, actually goes back 200 years, with an original flagstone floor to prove its antiquity, as well as wooden drawers running up to the ceiling, a relic of the days when bars doubled as grocery shops. Oliver St. John Gogarty accompanied W. B. Yeats here, in what was purportedly the latter's only visit to a pub.

COUNTY DUBLIN—SOUTHSIDE

JOHNNIE FOX'S (Glencullen, Co. Dublin, tel. 01/295–5647), 12 km (8 mi) from the city center, sits 1,000 ft up in the Dublin Mountains, making it the highest licensed premises in Ireland.

It's approached by a winding and steeply climbing road that turns off the main Dublin–Enniskerry road at Stepaside. Steadfastly refusing to bow to the whims of modernization, it has maintained all of its traditional character—oak tables, rough-stone floor flags strewn with sawdust, and ancient bric-a-brac, including copper kettles, crockery, old prints, and guns—appearing very much as it did in the early 19th century, when Daniel O'Connell used it as a safe house for his seditious meetings. Lunch and dinner are served; the specialty is seafood, which is alone worth the journey. In the evenings there is traditional Irish music.

TEMPLE BAR

The **FRONT LOUNGE** (33 Parliament St., Temple Bar, tel. 01/679–3988), a modern, well-appointed pub, caters to a mixed crowd of young professionals, both gay and straight.

OLIVER ST. JOHN GOGARTY (57 Fleet St., Temple Bar, tel. 01/671–1822) is a lively bar that attracts all ages and nationalities and overflows in summer. On most nights there is traditional Irish music upstairs.

PALACE BAR (21 Fleet St., Temple Bar, tel. 01/677–9290), scarcely changed over the past 60 years, is tiled and rather barren looking but popular with journalists and writers (the Irish Times is nearby). The walls are hung with cartoons drawn by the illustrators who used to spend time here.

Gay and Lesbian Pubs

The **GEORGE** (89 S. Great George's St., tel. 01/478–2983), Dublin's two-floor main gay pub, draws an almost entirely male crowd; its nightclub stays open until 2:30 AM nightly except Tuesday.

OUT ON THE LIFFEY (27 Ormond Quay, tel. 01/872–2480) is Dublin's second gay pub; it draws a mixed crowd of men and women.

Irish Cabaret

BALLSBRIDGE/SOUTH CITY CENTER

DOYLE BURLINGTON HOTEL (Upper Leeson St., tel. 01/660–5222) is a high-class lounge featuring a well-performed Irish cabaret, with dancing, music, and song.

JURYS HOTEL (Ballsbridge, tel. 01/660–5000) stages a cabaret show similar to that at the Doyle Burlington hotel (☞ *above*).

CITY CENTER

CASTLE INN (Christ Church Pl., tel. 01/475–1122) is really just a huge pub that has traditional Irish music and dancing with dinner in a medieval-style banquet hall.

COUNTY DUBLIN—NORTHSIDE

ABBEY TAVERN (Howth, tel. 01/839–0307) has a rip-roaring cabaret with rousing, traditional Irish songs.

CLONTARF CASTLE (Castle Ave., Clontarf, tel. 01/833–2321) offers a spectacular setting for a traditional night of song and comedy.

Irish Music and Dancing

SOUTH DUBLIN

COMHALTAS CEOLTÓIRI ÉIREANN (35 Belgrave Sq., Monkstown, tel. 01/280–0295) has boisterous summer evenings of genuine Irish music and dancing.

HARCOURT HOTEL (Harcourt St., tel. 01/478–3677) is where some of the best traditional musicians gather for wild jam sessions.

Nightclubs

The dominant sound in Dublin's nightclubs is electronic dance music, and the crowd that flocks to them every night of the week is of the trendy, under-25 generation. However, there are a couple of clubs where you're more likely to hear tango than techno, such as the weekend nightclub at the Gaiety Theatre, Thursday nights at the Pod, and Sunday nights at Lillie's Bordello. **Velure** (tel. 01/

670–3750) is one of Dublin's most successful nightclub promoters, organizing live music, DJs, and theme parties; call to find out what's going on.

CITY CENTER

The **DA CLUB** (3–5 Clarendon Market, tel. 01/670–5116), in the refurbished Dublin Arts Club, is one of the most popular spots in town. Despite its small capacity, it has a wide variety of nightly entertainment—from comedy acts to live bands to dance clubs—often running concurrently on its two floors. The venue attracts a young bohemian crowd. It has full bar facilities.

LEESON STREET—just off St. Stephen's Green and known as "the strip"—is a main nightclub area from pub closing time to 4 AM, although it has lost its gloss in recent years. Dress at these places is informal, but jeans and sneakers are not welcome. Most of these clubs are licensed only to sell wine, and the prices can be exorbitant (up to £20 for a mediocre bottle); the upside is that most don't charge to get in.

LILLIE'S BORDELLO (Grafton St., tel. 01/679–9204) is a popular spot for a trendy, professional crowd, as well as for rock and film stars. On Sunday nights, the strict dress code is relaxed for a night of live music and DJs.

The **POD** (Harcourt St., tel. 01/478–0166), also known as the "Place of Dance," is Dublin's most-renowned dance club, especially among the younger set. Entry is judged as much on clothing as on age; it helps to look either stylish or rich, except on Thursday nights, when the club hosts a no-frills, no-nonsense night of dance-floor jazz and funk.

The **RED BOX** (Old Harcourt St. Station, Harcourt St., tel. 01/478–0166), adjacent to the Pod (☞ *above*) and the Chocolate Bar, can pack in more than 1,000 people and surround them with state-of-the-art sound and light. It regularly hosts Irish and international rock acts as well as celebrity DJs from Europe and the United

States. As do most other Dublin rock venues, the Red Box has full bar facilities.

RÍ RA (Dame Ct., tel. 01/677–4835) is part of the hugely popular Globe bar (☞ *above*). The name means "uproar" in Irish, and on most nights the place does go a little wild. It's one of the best spots in Dublin for no-frills, fun dancing. Upstairs is more low key.

TEMPLE BAR

The **KITCHEN** (E. Essex St., tel. 01/677–6359) is in the basement of the Clarence hotel (☞ Where To Stay); its popularity, mainly with an under-30s crowd, owes much to its owners, Bono and the Edge of U2.

THE ARTS

Theater and popular music are the dominant performing arts in Dublin, but by no means the only ones; they are supplemented by a handful of cinemas, an opera company, classical music, art galleries, and the city's vibrant pub life.

Art Galleries

GREEN ON RED GALLERIES. This rather unprepossessing gallery, near the back of Trinity College, is one of Dublin's best, with constantly changing exhibitions featuring the work of some of the country's—and Britain's—most promising up-and-coming artists. *26–28 Lombard St. E, tel. 01/671–3414. Weekdays 11–6, Sat. 11–5.*

KERLIN GALLERY. Perhaps Dublin's most important commercial gallery, this large space behind Grafton Street exhibits the work of many of Ireland's most important contemporary artists, including such internationally recognized figures as New York–based Sean Scully, Kathy Prendergast, Paul Seawright, and Stephen McKenna. *Anne's La., S. Anne St., tel. 01/670–9093. Weekdays 10–5:45, Sat. 11–4:30.*

ORIGINAL PRINT GALLERY. An ultramodern building by the same prominent Dublin architect who designed Temple Bar Gallery

(☞ *below*), this place specializes in handmade, limited editions of prints by Irish artists. Also in the building, the **Black Church Print Studio** (tel. 01/677–3629) exhibits prints. *4 Temple Bar, tel. 01/677–3657. Tues.–Fri. 10:30–5:30, Sat. 11–5, Sun. 2–6.*

NATIONAL PHOTOGRAPHIC ARCHIVE. A real treasure trove of Irish photographs from the last century, the Archive also hosts exhibits of work from contemporary Irish photographers, North and South. *Temple Bar, tel. 01/603–0200. Mon.–Fri. 10–5, Sat. 10–2.*

RUBICON GALLERY. This second-floor gallery overlooking St. Stephen's Green holds a number of yearly exhibitions featuring work in all media from sculpture to photography. *10 St. Stephen's Green, tel. 01/670–8055. Mon.–Sat. 11–5:30.*

SOLOMON GALLERY. Not exactly a risk taker, the Solomon has slowly developed a name as one of Dublin's leading fine-art galleries. *Powerscourt Townhouse Centre, S. William St., tel. 01/679–4237. Mon.–Sat. 10–5:30.*

TEMPLE BAR GALLERY. A flagship of the Temple Bar redevelopment project, this gallery exhibits the work of emerging Irish photographers, painters, sculptors, and other artists in monthly rotating shows. *5–9 Temple Bar, tel. 01/671–0073. Mon.–Sat. 11–6, Sun. 2–6.*

Classical Music and Opera

The **BANK OF IRELAND ARTS CENTER** (Foster Pl. S, tel. 01/671–1488) is the perfect sport for a regular lunchtime recital.

NATIONAL CONCERT HALL (Earlsfort Terr., tel. 01/475–1666), just off St. Stephen's Green, is Dublin's main theater for classical music of all kinds, from symphonies to chamber groups. It's also home to the National Symphony Orchestra of Ireland.

OPERA IRELAND (John Player House, 276–288 S. Circular Rd., tel. 01/453–5519) performs at the Gaiety Theatre (☞ *below*); call to find out what's on and when.

ONE LAST TRAVEL TIP:

Pack an easy way to reach the world.

123 456 7891 2345
J.D. SMITH

Wherever you travel, the MCI WorldCom Card is the easiest way to stay in touch. You can use it to call to and from more than 125 countries worldwide. And you can earn bonus miles when you use your card. So go ahead, travel the world. MCI WorldCom makes it even more rewarding. For additional access codes, visit www.wcom.com/worldphone.

MCI WORLDCOM.

EASY TO CALL WORLDWIDE

1. Just dial the WorldPhone® access number of the country you're calling from.

2. Dial or give the operator your MCI WorldCom Card number.

3. Dial or give the number you're calling.

Belgium ◆	0800-10012
Czech Republic ◆	00-42-000112
Denmark ◆	8001-0022
France ◆	0-800-99-0019
Germany	0800-888-8000
Hungary ◆	06▼-800-01411
Ireland	1-800-55-1001
Italy ◆	172-1022
Mexico	01-800-021-8000
Netherlands ◆	0800-022-91-22
Spain	900-99-0014
Switzerland ◆	0800-89-0222
United Kingdom	0800-89-0222
United States	1-800-888-8000

◆ Public phones may require deposit of coin or phone card for dial tone. ▼ Wait for second dial tone.

EARN FREQUENT FLIER MILES

Bureau de change

Cambio

外国為替

In this city, you can find money on almost any street.

NO-FEE FOREIGN EXCHANGE

The Chase Manhattan Bank has over 80 convenient
locations near New York City destinations such as:

    Times Square
    Rockefeller Center
    Empire State Building
    2 World Trade Center
    United Nations Plaza

Exchange any of 75 foreign currencies

CHASE

THE RIGHT RELATIONSHIP IS EVERYTHING.®

OPERA THEATRE COMPANY (18 St. Andrew St., tel. 01/679–4962) is Ireland's only touring opera company, performing at venues in Dublin and throughout the country.

ROYAL HOSPITAL KILMAINHAM (Military Rd., tel. 01/671–8666) presents frequent classical concerts in its magnificent historic interior.

ST. STEPHEN'S CHURCH (Merrion Sq., tel. 01/288–0663) has a regular program of choral and orchestral events in its glorious setting.

Film

Dublin has two dozen cinema screens in the city center and a number of large, multiscreen cinema complexes in the suburbs, showing current releases made in Ireland and abroad.

IRISH FILM CENTRE (6 Eustace St., tel. 01/677–8788; ☞ Temple Bar in Here and There) shows classic and new independent films.

SAVOY CINEMA (O'Connell St., tel. 01/874–6000), just across from the General Post Office, is a four-screen theater with the largest screen in the country.

SCREEN CINEMA (2 Townsend St., tel. 01/671–4988), between Trinity College and O'Connell Street Bridge, is a popular three-screen art-house cinema.

VIRGIN MULTIPLEX (Parnell Center, Parnell St., tel. 01/872–8400), a 12-screen theater just off O'Connell Street, is the city center's only multiplex movie house and shows the latest commercial features.

Jazz

The **GLOBE** (11 S. Great George's St., tel. 01/671–1220) has live jazz on Sundays from 5 to 7 PM. The emphasis is on funk fusion and acid jazz, interspersed with classic '50s–'60s sounds. The quality of the music varies, and the audience is often less than attentive.

JJ SMYTH'S (12 Aungier St., tel. 01/475–2565) is an old-time jazz venue where Louis Stewart, the granddaddy of Irish jazz, has a regular slot.

PENDULUM CLUB (The Norseman, at Eustace St. and E. Essex St., Temple Bar) is the place to go for good jazz, with some of Ireland's top acts featured as well as guest appearances by internationally recognized musicians.

Rock and Contemporary Music

The long established **INTERNATIONAL BAR** (Wicklow St., tel. 01/677–9250) has a tiny, get-close-to-the band venue upstairs. It hosts theater in the afternoons.

MEAN FIDDLER (Wexford St., tel. 01/475–8555) is the small Dublin cousin of the famous London venue. There's plenty of room here for rising Irish and international acts who draw young, lively crowds. After the gig, there's usually a late-night club; your ticket gets you in free.

OLYMPIA THEATRE (72 Dame St., tel. 01/677–7744; ☞ Temple Bar in Here and There) puts on its "Midnight from the Olympia" shows every Friday and Saturday from midnight to 2 AM, with everything from rock to country.

THE POINT (Eastlink Br., tel. 01/836–3633), a 6,000-capacity arena about 1 km (½ mi) east of the Custom House on the Liffey, is Dublin's premier venue for internationally renowned acts. Call or send a self-addressed envelope to receive a list of upcoming shows; tickets can be difficult to obtain, so book early.

TEMPLE BAR MUSIC CENTRE (Curved St., tel. 01/670–0533)— a music venue, rehearsal space, television studio, and pub rolled into one—buzzes with activity every day of the week. Live acts range from rock bands to ethnic music to singer-songwriters.

WHELAN'S (25 Wexford St., tel. 01/478–0766), just off the southeastern corner of St. Stephen's Green, is one of the city's best—and most popular—music venues, featuring well-known acts performing everything from rock to folk to traditional.

Theater

ABBEY THEATRE (Lower Abbey St., tel. 01/878–7222), the home of Ireland's national theater company, stages mainstream, mostly Irish traditional, plays. Its sister theater at the same address, the **Peacock,** offers more experimental drama. W. B. Yeats and his patron, Lady Gregory, opened the theater in 1904, which became a major center for the Irish literary renaissance—the place that first staged works by J. M. Synge and Sean O'Casey, among many others. The original theater burned down in 1951, but it reopened with a modern design in 1966.

ANDREW'S LANE THEATRE (9–11 Andrew's La., tel. 01/679–5720) presents experimental productions.

GAIETY THEATRE (S. King St., tel. 01/677–1717) is the home of Opera Ireland (☞ *above*) when it's not showing musical comedy, drama, and revues.

GATE THEATRE (Cavendish Row, Parnell Sq., tel. 01/874–4045; ☞ North of the Liffey *in* Here and There), an intimate 371-seat theater in a jewel-like Georgian assembly hall, produces the classics and contemporary plays by leading Irish writers.

OLYMPIA THEATRE (72 Dame St., tel. 01/677–7744; ☞ Temple Bar *in* Here and There) is Dublin's oldest and premier multipurpose theatrical venue. In addition to its high-profile musical performances, it has seasons of comedy, vaudeville, and ballet.

PROJECT ARTS CENTRE (39 E. Essex St., tel. 01/671–2321) is an established fringe theater.

Not a Night Owl?

You can learn a lot about a place if you take its pulse after dark. So even if you're the original early-to-bed type, there's every reason to vary your routine when you're away from home.

EXPERIENCE THE FAMILIAR IN A NEW PLACE Whether your thing is going to the movies or going to concerts, it's always different away from home. In clubs, new faces and new sounds add up to a different scene. Or you may catch movies you'd never see at home.

TRY SOMETHING NEW Do something you've never done before. It's another way to dip into the local scene. A simple suggestion: Go out later than usual—go dancing late and finish up with breakfast at dawn.

DO SOMETHING OFFBEAT Look into lectures and readings as well as author appearances in book stores. You may even meet your favorite novelist.

EXPLORE A DAYTIME NEIGHBORHOOD AT NIGHT Take a nighttime walk through an explorable area you've already seen by day. You'll get a whole different view of it.

ASK AROUND If you strike up a conversation with like-minded people during the course of your day, ask them about their favorite spots. Your hotel concierge is another resource.

DON'T WING IT As soon as you've nailed down your travel dates, look into local publications or surf the Net to see what's on the calendar while you're in town. Look for hot regional acts, dance and theater, big-name performing artists, expositions, and sporting events. Then call or click to order tickets.

CHECK OUT THE NEIGHBORHOOD Whenever you don't know the neighborhood you'll be visiting, review safety issues with people in your hotel. What's the transportation situation? Can you walk there, or do you need a cab? Is there anything else you need to know?

CASH OR CREDIT? Know before you go. It's always fun to be surprised—but not when you can't cover your check.

SAMUEL BECKETT CENTRE (Trinity College, tel. 01/608–2266) is home to Trinity's Drama Department as well as visiting groups from around Europe. Dance is often featured.

TIVOLI (135–138 Francis St., tel. 01/454–4472) brings culture to the heart of old working-class Dublin, the Liberties. Lighter, comedy-based shows and the occasional Shakespeare play are favored.

In This Chapter

Updated by Anto Howard

where to stay

"AN ABSOLUTE AVALANCHE OF NEW HOTELS" is how the *Irish Times* characterized Dublin's hotel boom. It's unlikely that there have ever been more hotels under construction at one time in the capital than there are now, while at the same time, at least one-quarter of the existing hotels are being renovated. New lodgings have sprung up in all areas of the city, including the much-talked-about one in Smithfield, and some in Ballsbridge, an inner "suburb" that's a 20-minute walk from the city center. Demand for rooms means that rates are still high at the best hotels by the standards of any major European or American city (and factoring in the exchange rate means a hotel room can take a substantial bite out of any traveler's budget). Service charges range from 15% in expensive hotels to zero in moderate and inexpensive ones. Be sure to inquire when you make reservations.

Many hotels have a weekend, or "B&B," rate that's often 30%–40% cheaper than the ordinary rate; some hotels also have a midweek special that provides discounts of up to 35%. These rates are available throughout the year but are harder to get in high season. Ask about them when booking a room (they are available only on a prebooked basis), especially if you plan a brief or weekend stay. If you've rented a car and you're not staying at a hotel with secure parking facilities, it's worth considering a location out of the city center, such as Dalkey or Killiney, where the surroundings are more pleasant and you won't have to worry about parking on city streets, which can be difficult.

Dublin has a decent selection of less-expensive accommodations—including many moderately priced hotels with basic but agreeable rooms. As rule, lodgings on the northside of the river tend to be more affordable than those on the south. Many B&Bs, long the mainstay of the economy end of the market, have upgraded their facilities and now provide rooms with private bathrooms or showers, as well as multichannel color televisions and direct-dial telephones, for around £25 a night per person. B&Bs tend to be in suburban areas—generally a 10-minute bus ride from the center of the city. This is not in itself a great drawback, and savings can be significant.

CATEGORY	COST*
$$$$	over £180
$$$	£140–£180
$$	£100–£140
$	under £100

*All prices are for a standard double room, including tax, in high season

CITY CENTER (SOUTHSIDE)

$$$$ **CONRAD DUBLIN INTERNATIONAL.** In a seven-story redbrick and smoked-glass building just off St. Stephen's Green, the Conrad, owned by the Hilton Group, is firmly aimed at international business travelers. Gleaming, light marble graces the large, formal lobby. Rooms are rather cramped and have uninspiring views of the adjacent office buildings, but they are nicely outfitted with natural wood furnishings, painted in sand colors and pastel greens, and graced with Spanish marble in the bathrooms. A note to light sleepers: the air-conditioning/heating system can be noisy. The hotel has two restaurants: the informal Plurabelle and the plusher Alexandra Room. The main bar, Alfie Byrne's, named in honor of Dublin's lord mayor for most of the 1930s (a renowned teetotaller), attempts to re-create a traditional Irish pub atmosphere. *Earlsfort Terr., Dublin 2, tel. 01/676–5555, 800/HILTONS*

in the U.S., fax 01/676–5424. 182 rooms with bath, 9 suites. 2 restaurants, bar, in-room data ports, in-room safes, in-room VCRs, minibars, no-smoking floor, no-smoking rooms, room service, exercise room, concierge, business services, meeting rooms, free parking. AE, DC, MC, V. www.conradinternational.ie

$$$$ FITZWILLIAM HOTEL. A relative newcomer to the luxury circuit, the Fitzwilliam has been dubbed a "designer" hotel for its impeccable decor: everything from light fixtures to luggage racks to staff uniforms is the work of international design leaders. The modern glass building has a large roof garden and overlooks the park. The spacious rooms are furnished in a contemporary, comfortable style. Conrad Gallagher, one of Ireland's young up-and-coming chefs, presides over the rooftop restaurant. St. Stephen's Green, Dublin 2, tel. 01/478–7000, fax 01/478–7878. 135 rooms with bath, 2 suites. Restaurant, bar, brasserie, in-room data ports, no-smoking rooms, room service, exercise room, laundry service, business services, meeting rooms. AE, DC, MC, V. www.fitzwilliamh.com

$$$$ MERRION. The home of Arthur Wellesley, the Duke of Wellington
★   and hero of the Battle of Waterloo, is one of four exactingly restored Georgian town houses that make up part of this luxurious hotel. The stately rooms are richly appointed in classic Georgian style down to the last detail—from the crisp linen sheets to the Carrara marble bathrooms. Some are vaulted with delicate Adamesque plasterwork ceilings, and others are graced with magnificent, original marble fireplaces. The Garden Wing, at the back of the hotel behind the elegant gardens laid out by Irish landscape designer Jim Reynolds, has smaller rooms than the main house, but they are just as ornate. You know this place has to be one of Dublin's best—after all, leading Dublin restaurateur Patrick Guilbaud (☞ Eating Out) moved his eponymous restaurant here. Upper Merrion St., Dublin 2, tel. 01/603–0600, fax 01/603–0700. 127 rooms with bath, 18 suites. 2 restaurants, 2 bars, in-room data ports, in-room safes, in-room VCRs, minibars, no-smoking floor, no-smoking rooms, room service, indoor pool, barbershop, beauty salon, massage, steam

room, dry cleaning, laundry service, concierge, business services, meeting rooms, free parking. AE, DC, MC, V. www.merrionhotel.com

$$$$ **SHELBOURNE MÉRIDIEN HOTEL.** Paris has the Ritz, New York has
★ the Plaza, and Dublin has the Shelbourne. The grand old history (Ireland's constitution was signed in Room 112 in 1921) of this grand old place was written by no less than celebrated novelist and wit Elizabeth Bowen. One step past the ornate, redbrick and white-gingerbread facade and you know you're in Dublin: Waterford chandeliers, gleaming Old Masters on the wall, and Irish Chippendale chairs invite you to linger in the lobby—as many fabled names have done so since this city showplace opened in 1824 (☞ The Center City: Around Trinity College in Here and There). Each guest room is unique; all have fine, carefully selected furniture and luxurious drapes, with splendid antiques in the older rooms. Those in front overlook St. Stephen's Green, but rooms in the back, without a view, are quieter. The impressive suites have separate sitting rooms and dressing areas. The restaurant, 27 The Green, is one of the most elegant rooms in Dublin; Lord Mayor's Lounge, off the lobby, is a perfect rendezvous spot and offers a lovely afternoon tea—a real Dublin tradition. *27 St. Stephen's Green, Dublin 2, tel. 01/676–6471, 800/543–4300 in the U.S., fax 01/661–6006. 194 rooms with bath, 9 suites. 2 restaurants, 2 bars, indoor pool, hot tub, sauna, health club, free parking. AE, DC, MC, V. www.shelbourne.ie*

$$$$ **WESTBURY.** This comfortable, modern hotel is in the heart of southside Dublin, right off the city's buzzing shopping mecca, Grafton Street. Join elegantly dressed Dubliners for afternoon tea in the spacious mezzanine-level main lobby, furnished with antiques. Alas, the utilitarian rooms—painted in pastels—don't share the lobby's elegance. More inviting are the suites, which combine European decor with tasteful Japanese screens and prints. The flowery Russell Room serves formal lunches and dinners; the downstairs Sandbank, a seafood restaurant and bar, has decor resembling a Joycean-period establishment. *Grafton St.,*

Dublin 2, tel. 01/679–1122, fax 01/679–7078. *203 rooms with bath, 8 suites. 2 restaurants, bar, minibars, no-smoking rooms, room service, dry cleaning, laundry service, free parking. AE, DC, MC, V.*

$$$ DAVENPORT, MONT CLARE, AND ALEXANDER. The Davenport's gorgeous, bright-yellow neoclassic facade was built in the 1860s to front a church, but a 1993 conversion remade the building into this hotel, just behind Trinity College. The reasonably spacious rooms and larger suites are fitted in tasteful, deep colors and functional furnishings. The hotel restaurant, Lanyon's, serves breakfast, lunch, and dinner amid traditional Georgian decor. In the comfortable President's Bar, see how many heads of state you can identify in the photos covering the walls. *Merrion Sq., Dublin 2, tel. 01/661–6800, 800/327–0200 in the U.S., fax 01/661–5663. 118 rooms with bath, 2 suites. Restaurant, bar, air-conditioning, in-room VCRs, minibars, no-smoking rooms, room service, dry cleaning, laundry service, concierge, business services, meeting rooms, free parking. AE, DC, MC, V.*

$$ CENTRAL HOTEL. Established in 1887, this grand, old-style redbrick hotel is in the heart of the center city, steps from Grafton Street, Temple Bar, and Dublin Castle. Rooms are small but have high ceilings and practical but tasteful furniture. Adjacent to the hotel is Molly Malone's Tavern, a lively hotel-bar with plenty of regulars who come for the atmosphere and the live, traditional Irish music on Friday and Saturday nights. The restaurant and Library Bar—one of the best spots in the city for a quiet pint—are on the first floor. *1–5 Exchequer St., Dublin 2, tel. 01/679–7302, fax 01/679–7303. 67 rooms with bath, 3 suites. Restaurant, 2 bars, room service, dry cleaning, laundry service, concierge, business services, meeting rooms. AE, DC, MC, V. www.centralhotel.ie*

$$ DRURY COURT HOTEL. A two-minute walk from Grafton Street and just around the corner from some of the city's best restaurants, this small hotel opened in March 1996. Rooms are done in subtle greens, golds, and burgundies. The parquet-floored rathskeller dining room serves breakfast and dinner; lunch is served in the casual Digges Lane Bar, frequented by many young Dubliners. 28–30 Lower Stephens St., Dublin 2, tel. 01/475–1988, fax 01/478–5730. 30 rooms with bath, 2 suites. Restaurant, bar, room service, dry cleaning, laundry service, meeting room. AE, DC, MC, V. indigo.ie/ ˜ druryct/

$$ STEPHEN'S HALL ALL-SUITE. Dublin's only all-suite hotel is in a tastefully modernized Georgian town house just off Stephen's Green. The suites, considerably larger than the average hotel room, include one or two bedrooms, a separate sitting room, a fully equipped kitchen, and bath. They are comfortably equipped with quality modern furniture. Top-floor suites have spectacular city views, and ground-floor suites have private entrances. Morel's Restaurant serves breakfast, lunch, and dinner. 14–17 Lower Leeson St., Dublin 2, tel. 01/661–0585, fax 01/661–0606. 37 suites. Restaurant, 2 bars, room service, no-smoking rooms, meeting rooms, free parking. AE, DC, MC, V.

$ AVALON HOUSE. Many young, independent travelers rate this cleverly restored, Victorian redbrick building the most appealing of Dublin's hostels. A 2-minute walk from Grafton Street and 5–10 minutes from some of the city's best music venues, the hostel has a mix of dormitories, rooms without bath, and rooms with bath. The dorm rooms and en-suite quads all have loft areas that offer more privacy than you'd typically find in a multibed room. The Avalon Café serves food until 10 PM but is open as a common room after hours. 55 Aungier St., Dublin 2, tel. 01/475–0001, fax 01/475–0303. 35 4-bed rooms with bath, 5 4-bed rooms without bath, 4 twin rooms with bath, 4 single rooms without bath, 22 twin rooms without bath, 5 12-bed dorms, 1 10-bed dorm, 1 26-bed dorm. Bar, café. AE, MC, V. www.avalon-house.ie

$ JURYS CHRISTCHURCH INN. Expect few frills at this functional budget hotel, part of a Jurys minichain that offers a low, fixed room rate for up to three adults or two adults and two children. (The **Jurys Custom House Inn** [Custom House Quay, Dublin 1, tel. 01/

607–5000, fax 01/829–0400], at the International Financial Services Centre, operates according to the same plan.) The biggest plus is the pleasant location, facing Christ Church Cathedral and within walking distance of most city-center attractions. The rather spartan rooms are decorated in pastel colors and utilitarian furniture. *Christ Church Pl., Dublin 8, tel. 01/454–0000, fax 01/454–0012. 182 rooms with bath. Restaurant, bar, no-smoking rooms, parking (fee). AE, DC, MC, V. www.jurys.com*

$ **KILRONAN HOUSE.** A five-minute walk from St. Stephen's Green,
★ Deirdre and Noel Comer's guest house is a favorite—thanks in large measure to the friendly welcome. The large, late-19th-century terraced house, with a white facade, was carefully converted, and the furnishings are updated each year. Richly patterned wallpaper and carpets grace guest rooms, while orthopedic beds (rather rare in Dublin hotels, let alone guest houses) help to guarantee a restful night's sleep. If you have a dog back home whom you're pining after, you'll appreciate Homer, the Labrador. *70 Adelaide Rd., Dublin 2, tel. 01/475–5266, fax 01/478–2841. 12 rooms with bath. Free parking. MC, V.*

$ **NUMBER 31.** Two Georgian mews strikingly renovated in the early '60s as the private home of Sam Stephenson, Ireland's leading modern architect, are now connected via a small garden to the grand town house they once served. Together they form a marvelous guest house a short walk from St. Stephen's Green. Owners Deirdre and Noel Comer, who also own Kilronan House (☞ *above*), serve made-to-order breakfasts at refectory tables in the balcony dining room. The white-tiled sunken living room, with its black leather sectional sofa and modern artwork that includes a David Hockney print, will make you think you're in California, not Dublin. *31 Leeson Close, Dublin 2, tel. 01/676–5011, fax 01/676–2929. 18 rooms with bath. No-smoking rooms, dry cleaning, laundry service, free parking. AE, MC, V.*

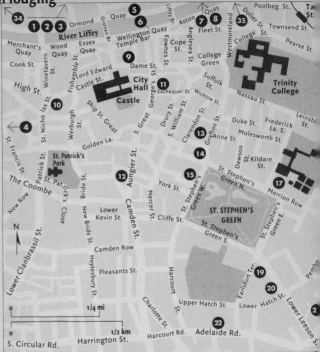

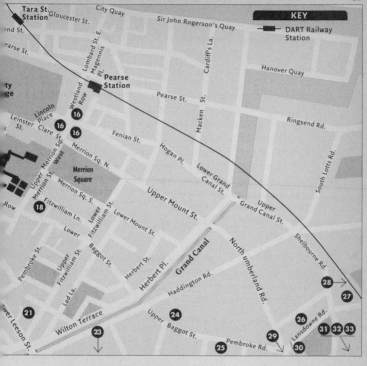

TEMPLE BAR

$$$$ THE CLARENCE. You might well bump into celebrity friends of co-owners Bono and the Edge of U2 at this contemporary hotel, understated to the point of austerity. Stone floors, unadorned oak wainscoting, and a leather-lined elevator set the slightly chaotic tone downstairs, where the Octagon Bar and the Tea Room Restaurant are popular Temple Bar watering holes. Guest rooms are done in a mishmash of earth tones accented with deep purple, gold, cardinal red, and royal blue. With the exception of those in the penthouse suite, rooms are small; but *very* comfortable beds, sparkling bathrooms, and views of the Liffey, from the front rooms, compensate. The laissez-faire service seems to take its cue from the minimalist decor, so if you like to be pampered, stay elsewhere. *6–8 Wellington Quay, Dublin 2, tel. 01/670–9000, fax 01/670–7800. 46 rooms with bath, 4 suites. Restaurant, bar, no-smoking rooms, minibars, dry cleaning, laundry service, meeting rooms, free parking. AE, DC, MC, V.*

$$ ARLINGTON HOTEL. A converted auction house on the quays is the setting for this privately owned boutique hotel. Pass between the gold lions guarding the door and enter a medieval great hall with suits of armor, sumptuous swags, and creaky floors. The theme continues in the bar; boisterous and echo-filled, it's more mead hall than cozy pub. Rich upholstery, romantic lighting, and hearty Irish fare (full breakfast is included in the rates) make the restaurant more intimate. Upstairs the corridors and rooms have a Georgian feel, with soothing pastel yellow or lavender walls; spreads and drapes are awash in golds, rusts, and blues and have patterns and details evocative of tapestries. The hotel also has limited off-street parking, though your way might be blocked by a Guinness truck. *23–25 Bachelor's Walk, O'Connell Bridge, Dublin 1, tel. 01/804–9100, fax 01/804–9112. 115 rooms with bath. Restaurant, bar, in-room data ports, no-smoking rooms, dance club, baby-sitting, laundry service, meeting rooms, free parking. AE, DC, MC, V.*

$$ PARLIAMENT. Although the Parliament is in one of Dublin's finest Edwardian buildings, its interior is very much functional, if tidy, and attracts a mostly business clientele. They are drawn by the location, on Dame Street near the Central Bank and a few blocks down from Trinity College. Rooms are a good size, with a simple, slightly monotonous beige and off-white scheme. The Senate Restaurant and Forum Bar keep up the democratic theme. *Lord Edward St., Dublin 2, tel. 01/670–8777, fax 01/670–8787. 63 rooms with bath. Restaurant, bar, no-smoking rooms. AE, DC, MC, V.*

$$ TEMPLE BAR. In a former bank building just around the corner from Trinity College, this hotel has an Art Deco lobby with a large and old-fashioned cast-iron fireplace, natural-wood furniture, and lots of plants. Off the lobby are a small cocktail bar and the bright, open, glass-roofed Terrace Restaurant, which serves sandwiches, pastas, omelets, and fish all day. Mahogany furnishings and autumn green and rust colors adorn guest rooms, nearly all of which have double beds, making them more than a little cramped. The Boomerang nightclub on the premises is open to both guests and the public. *Fleet St., Dublin 2, tel. 01/677–3333, fax 01/677–3088. 129 rooms with bath, 1 suite. Restaurant, 2 bars, nightclub, parking (fee). AE, DC, MC, V.*

SOUTH CITY CENTER—BALLSBRIDGE

$$$$ BERKELEY COURT. The most quietly elegant of Dublin's large modern hotels, Berkeley Court has a glass-and-concrete exterior designed in a modern, blocklike style set in verdant grounds. Inside, the vast white-tiled and plushly carpeted lobby has roomy sofas and antique planters. The large rooms are decorated in golds, yellows, and greens, with antiques or reproductions of period furniture; bathrooms are tiled in marble. The five luxury suites have a Jacuzzi. The Berkeley Room restaurant has table d'hôte and à la carte menus; the more informal Conservatory Grill, with large windows, serves grilled food and snacks. *Lansdowne Rd., Dublin 4, tel. 01/660–1711, 800/550–0000 in the U.S., fax 01/661–7238. 157 rooms* with bath, 29 suites. 2 restaurants, bar, room service, no-smoking rooms, barbershop, beauty salon, exercise room, shops, dry cleaning, laundry service, business services, meeting rooms, free parking. AE, DC, MC, V.

$$$$ HERBERT PARK HOTEL. The Herbert Park sits adjacent to a park of the same name and beside the River Dodder. The large lobby has floor-to-ceiling windows and a slanted glass roof. The spacious bar, terrace lounge, and restaurant are Japanese-inspired. Relaxing shades of blue and cream predominate in the nicely sized rooms, which are brightened by green, red, or white bedspreads; all have individually controlled air-conditioning, a large desk, and two telephone lines. Some look onto the park. Two of the suites have large balconies with views of the park or the leafy suburbs. The restaurant has a large terrace where you can dine in warm weather. *Ballsbridge, Dublin 4, tel. 01/667–2200, fax 01/667–2595. 150 rooms with bath, 3 suites. Restaurant, bar, exercise room, business services, free parking. AE, DC, MC, V. www.herbertparkhotel.ie*

$$$$ JURYS AND THE TOWERS. These adjacent seven-story hotels, a short cab ride from the center of town, are popular with businesspeople and vacationers. They have more atmosphere than most comparable modern hotels, though the Towers has an edge over Jurys, its older (it dates from 1962), larger, less-expensive companion. Jurys has large, plainly decorated rooms with light walls and brown drapes; furnishings are functional but uninspired. The Towers' rooms are a third larger than those of Jurys, decorated in blue and gold with built-in, natural wood furniture; the large beds and armchairs are comfortable. All the suites in both hotels have their own sitting rooms and kitchenettes. The Dubliners Bar, modeled on an old country kitchen, is popular with upwardly mobile locals and guests. *Ballsbridge, Dublin 4, tel. 01/660–5000, fax 01/660–5540. Jurys: 288 rooms with bath, 3 suites; the Towers: 100 rooms with bath, 4 suites with kitchenettes. Restaurant, coffee shop, 2 bars, indoor-outdoor pool, hot tub, shop, cabaret (May–Oct.), dry cleaning, laundry service, business services, meeting rooms, free parking. AE, DC, MC, V. jurys.com*

$$$ DOYLE BURLINGTON. Dublin's largest hotel, popular with American tour groups and Irish and European business travelers, is about five minutes by car from the city center. Its impersonal, 1972 glass-and-concrete facade contrasts with the friendly and attentive staff. Public rooms, especially the large bar, have mahogany counters and hanging plants that enhance the conservatory-style setting. The generous-size rooms, in the usual modern plush in neutral tones, have large picture windows. At night, Annabel's nightclub and the seasonal Irish cabaret are both lively spots. Although the Burlington has no sports and health facilities, the Doyle hotel group (☞ Doyle Tara, *below*) has an arrangement that allows you to use the RiverView Sports Club in nearby Clonskeagh for £5 a visit. *Upper Leeson St., Dublin 4, tel. 01/660–5222, fax 01/660–8496. 523 rooms with bath. 2 restaurants, 3 bars, room service, shops, cabaret (May–Oct.), nightclub, dry cleaning, laundry service, business service, meeting rooms, free parking. AE, DC, MC, V.*

$$$ ★ HIBERNIAN. Only a 15-minute walk from the city center, this early 20th-century Edwardian nurses' home designed by Albert E. Murray—one of the architects of the Rotunda Hospital—is now a small luxury hotel. One of the city's most elegant and intimate hostelries, it has retained the distinctive red-and-amber brick facade and has smallish rooms, nicely done in pastels, with deep-pile carpets and comfortable furniture. The public rooms, in cheerful chintz and stripes, include a period-style library and a sun lounge—both comfortable spaces to relax before or after a dinner in the hotel's intimate restaurant, the Patrick Kavanagh Room. Amid all this Victorian elegance, the owners haven't forgotten the warming touches. *Eastmoreland Pl. off Upper Baggot St., Dublin 4, tel. 01/668–7666 or 800/414243, fax 01/660–2655. 40 rooms with bath. Restaurant, bar, parking (fee). AE, DC, MC, V.*

$$ ★ LANSDOWNE. This small Ballsbridge hotel has cozy rooms in Georgian style with deep floral-pattern decor. Photos of sports personalities hang on the walls of the Green Blazer bar in the basement, a popular haunt for local businesspeople and fans of the international rugby matches held at nearby Lansdowne Road; you can get a bite to eat here all day. Next to the bar is Parker's Restaurant, which specializes in seafood and grilled steaks. *27 Pembroke Rd., Dublin 4, tel. 01/668–2522, fax 01/668–5585. 37 rooms with bath, 2 suites. Restaurant, bar, free parking. AE, DC, MC, V.*

$ ★ **ARIEL GUEST HOUSE.** This redbrick, 1850 Victorian guest house is one of Dublin's finest, just a few steps from a DART stop and a 15-minute walk from St. Stephen's Green. Recently restored rooms in the main house are lovingly decorated with Victorian and Georgian antiques, Victoriana, and period wallpaper and drapes. The 13 rooms at the back of the house are more spartan, but all are immaculate. A Waterford-crystal chandelier hangs over the comfortable leather and mahogany furniture in the gracious, fireplace-warmed drawing room. Owner Michael O'Brien is an extraordinarily helpful and gracious host. *52 Lansdowne Rd., Dublin 4, tel. 01/668–5512, fax 01/668–5845. 40 rooms with bath. Breakfast room, free parking. MC, V.*

$ **MOUNT HERBERT HOTEL.** This sprawling accommodation is made up of a number of large Victorian-era houses. It overlooks some of Ballsbridge's fine rear gardens and is right near the main rugby stadium; the nearby DART will have you in the city center in seven minutes. The simple rooms are painted in light shades and contain little besides beds, but all have bathrooms and 10-channel TVs. You can relax in the lounge; the large restaurant, overlooking the English-style back garden (floodlit at night) and children's play area, serves three meals a day, with unpretentious dinners of steaks and stews. *7 Herbert Rd., Dublin 4, tel. 01/668–4321, fax 01/660–7077. 200 rooms with bath. Restaurant, bar, sauna, shop, business services, meeting rooms, free parking. AE, DC, MC, V. mountherberthotel.ie*

CITY CENTER (NORTHSIDE)

$$$$ **THE MORRISON.** Halfway between the Ha'penny and Capel Street bridges, it's no more than 10 minutes from Trinity College. The highly modern interior—designed by John Rocha, Ireland's

most acclaimed fashion designer—can be a bit cold. He had the last word on everything down to the toiletries and staff uniforms. Rooms are standard in decor but high-tech, with top-of-the-line entertainment units, satellite TV, and ISDN lines. The Halo restaurant (☞ Eating Out) has an Asian theme. *Ormond Quay, Dublin 1, tel. 01/879–2999 or 800/447–7462, fax 01/878–3185. 88 rooms with bath, 7 suites. 2 restaurants, 2 bars, in-room data ports, in-room VCRs, minibars, no-smoking rooms, room service, dry cleaning, laundry service, concierge, business services, meeting rooms, free parking. AE, DC, MC, V. morrisonhotel.ie*

$$ CHIEF O'NEILL'S. Named after a 19th-century Corkman who became chief of police in Chicago, Dublin's newest hotel dominates Smithfield Village. It is part of the complex that also houses Ceol (☞ Here and There), the traditional music museum. Like the museum, the hotel has a modern design, with a huge lobby-bar area overlooking a cobbled courtyard. Smallish, high-tech rooms all have ISDN lines and thoroughly up-to-date decor with chrome fixtures and minimalist furnishings. Top-floor suites have delightful roof-top gardens with views of the city on both sides of the Liffey. The café-bar has live traditional music and contemporary Irish food, and Asian cuisine is available in Kelly & Ping, a bright, airy restaurant off Duck Lane, an integral shopping arcade. *Smithfield Village, Dublin 7, tel. 01/817–3838, fax 01/817–3839. 70 rooms with bath, 3 suites. Restaurant, bar, in-room data ports, minibars, no-smoking rooms, room service, in-room VCRs, exercise room, shops, dry cleaning, laundry service, free parking. AE, DC, MC, V. chiefoneills.com*

$$ ROYAL DUBLIN HOTEL. O'Connell Street is not what it once was, but this renovated, quality hotel has just about a perfect location at the top of the old thoroughfare. All of the northside's major attractions are nearby, and you can walk south to Trinity College in 10 minutes. The public spaces are all well lit glass and brass, rooms are spacious, and the hotel has a reputation for extra friendly service. The Georgian Room and Raffles bar try to put on posh English airs, but the casual warmth of the Irish manages to heat up the slightly stuffy atmosphere. *O'Connell St., Dublin 1, tel. 01/873–3666, fax 01/873–3120. 117 rooms with bath, 3 suites. Restaurant, bar, in-room data ports, in-room VCRs, minibars, no-smoking rooms, room service, dry cleaning, laundry service. AE, MC, V. royaldublin.com*

$ DUBLIN INTERNATIONAL YOUTH HOSTEL. In a converted convent, Dublin's major hostel has a total of 420 beds divided between private rooms and dorm rooms with 8, 12, 15, or 22 beds. Bathroom facilities are communal, even for private rooms. This is a spartan, low-cost alternative to hotels; if you're not a member of the International Youth Hostel organization, you can stay for a small extra charge. The hostel is north of Parnell Square, near the Mater Hospital. *51 Mountjoy St., Dublin 1, tel. 01/830–1766, fax 01/380–1600. 2 twin rooms, 3 3-bed rooms, 2 4-bed rooms, 9 6-bed rooms, and 8-, 12-, 15-, and 22-bed dorms. Restaurant. MC, V.*

SOUTH COUNTY DUBLIN SUBURBS

$$$ DOYLE TARA. On the main coast road 10–15 minutes from the Dun Laoghaire ferry terminal and 6½ km (4 mi) from the city center, this unpretentious, informal seven-story hotel is also near the Booterstown Marsh Bird Sanctuary. The best rooms are in the original section and face Dublin Bay; rooms in the addition have slightly more modern decor. The restaurant serves grilled fish, steaks, and omelets. The hotel staff is very personable. *Merrion Rd., Dublin 4, tel. 01/269–4666, fax 01/269–1027. 114 rooms with bath. Restaurant, bar, no-smoking rooms, dry cleaning, laundry service, free parking. AE, DC, MC, V.*

$$$ ROYAL MARINE. This 1870 seaside hotel has been completely modernized. The comfortable, capacious rooms have also been refurbished with contemporary decor, though the eight suites with four-poster beds and sitting rooms preserve the lofty ceilings of the original building. Ask for a room at the front of the hotel, facing Dun Laoghaire harbor. *Marine Rd., Dun Laoghaire, Co. Dublin, tel. 01/280–1911, fax 01/280–1089. 95 rooms with bath, 8 suites. Restaurant,*

2 bars, room service, no-smoking rooms, business services, free parking. AE, DC, MC, V.

$$ FITZPATRICK CASTLE DUBLIN. ★ With its sweeping views over Dun Laoghaire and Dublin Bay, the Fitzpatrick is worth the 15-km (9-mi) drive from the city center. The original part of the hotel is an 18th-century stone castle, with a substantial modern addition housing rooms; many are furnished with antiques and four-poster beds and have large bathrooms. The hotel is convenient to golfing, horseback riding, and fishing; the fitness facilities include an 82-ft heated pool. The views from Killiney Hill, behind the hotel, are spectacular; the seaside village of Dalkey and Killiney Beach are both in walking distance. *Killiney, Co. Dublin, tel. 01/284–0700, fax 01/285–0207. 113 rooms with bath. Restaurant, bar, indoor pool, sauna, steam room, health club, meeting rooms, free parking. AE, DC, MC, V.*

$ BEWLEYS AT NEWLANDS CROSS. On the southwest outskirts of the city, this 1998 four-story hotel is a good option if you're planning to head out of the city (especially to points in the Southwest and West) early and don't want to deal with morning traffic. The hotel is emulating the formula recently made popular by Jurys Inns, in which rooms—here each has a double bed, a single bed, and a sofa bed—are a flat rate for up to three adults or two adults and two children. *Newlands Cross, Naas Rd., Dublin 22, tel. 01/464–0140, fax 01/464–0900. 200 rooms with bath. Café, free parking. AE, MC, V. bewleyshotels.com*

DUBLIN AIRPORT

$$$ FORTE POSTHOUSE. The only hotel at Dublin Airport, this low-rise, redbrick structure with a plain exterior has rooms that are basic but spacious. The Bistro Restaurant serves fish and meat entrées, as well as a selection of vegetarian dishes; Sampans serves Chinese cuisine at dinner only. There's live music in the bar on weekends. You have access to a nearby health club. *Dublin Airport, tel. 01/844–4211, fax 01/844–6002. 249 rooms with bath. 2 restaurants, bar, room service, free parking. AE, DC, MC, V.*

Hotel How-Tos

Where you stay does make a difference. Do you prefer a modern high-rise or an intimate B&B? A center-city location or the quiet suburbs? What facilities do you want? Sort through your priorities, then price it all out.

HOW TO GET A DEAL After you've chosen a likely candidate or two, phone them directly and price a room for your travel dates. Then call the hotel's toll-free number and ask the same questions. Also try consolidators and hotel-room discounters. You won't hear the same rates twice. On the spot, make a reservation as soon as you are quoted a price you want to pay.

PROMISES, PROMISES If you have special requests, make them when you reserve. Get written confirmation of any promises.

SETTLE IN Upon arriving, make sure everything works — lights and lamps, TV and radio, sink, tub, shower, and anything else that matters. Report any problems immediately. And don't wait until you need extra pillows or blankets or an ironing board to call housekeeping. Also check out the fire emergency instructions. Know where to find the fire exits, and make sure your companions do, too.

IF YOU NEED TO COMPLAIN Be polite but firm. Explain the problem to the person in charge. Suggest a course of action. If you aren't satisfied, repeat your requests to the manager. Document everything: Take pictures and keep a written record of who you've spoken with, when, and what was said. Contact your travel agent, if he made the reservations.

KNOW THE SCORE When you go out, take your hotel's business cards (one for everyone in your party). If you have extras, you can give them out to new acquaintances who want to call you.

TIP UP FRONT For special services, a tip or partial tip in advance can work wonders.

USE ALL THE HOTEL RESOURCES A concierge can make difficult things easy. But a desk clerk, bellhop, or other hotel employee who's friendly, smart, and ambitious can often steer you straight as well. A gratuity is in order if the advice is helpful.

$$ DOYLE SKYLON. This modern, five-story hotel with a concrete-and-glass facade is on the main road into Dublin city center from the airport. The generous-size rooms are plainly decorated in cool pastels; double beds and a pair of easy chairs are almost the only furniture. A glass-fronted lobby with a large bar and the Rendezvous Room restaurant dominate the public areas. The cooking is adequate but uninspired, with dishes such as grilled steak, poached cod, and omelets. *Upper Drumcondra Rd., Dublin 9, tel. 01/837–9121, fax 01/837–2778. 88 rooms with bath. Restaurant, bar, free parking. AE, DC, MC, V.*

PRACTICAL INFORMATION

Air Travel

CARRIERS

Aer Lingus is the national flag carrier of Ireland, with regularly scheduled flights to Shannon and Dublin from JFK, Newark, Boston's Logan, Chicago's O'Hare, and LAX. Delta has a daily departure from Atlanta that flies first to Dublin and on to Shannon. Continental flies daily direct to Dublin and Shannon, departing from Newark Airport in New Jersey. Aeroflot flies twice weekly from Miami, three times weekly from Washington, DC (Dulles), and once a week from Chicago. With the exception of special offers, the prices of the four airlines tend to be similar.

London to Dublin is now one of the busiest international air routes in the world and four main carriers, as well as numerous smaller airlines, provide daily service on this route. With such healthy competition, there are plenty of bargains to be found. Ryanair, a relatively new Irish airline, is famous for its cheap, no-frills service.

➤ MAJOR AIRLINES: **Aer Lingus** (tel. 800/223–6537). **Aeroflot** (tel. 888/340–6400). **Continental** (tel. 800/231–0856). **Delta** (tel. 800/241–4141).

➤ FROM THE U.K.: **Aer Lingus** (tel. 0845/973–7747 or 020/8899–4747). **British Airways** (tel. 0345/222–1111). **British Midlands** (tel. 020/8745–7321). **Ryanair** (tel. 0870/156–9569).

Airports and Transfers

Dublin Airport, 10 km (6 mi) north of the city center, serves international and domestic airlines.

➤ AIRPORT INFORMATION: **Dublin Airport** (tel. 01/844–4900).

AIRPORT SHUTTLE

Dublin Bus operates a shuttle service between Dublin Airport and the city center with departures outside the arrivals gateway;

pay the driver inside the coach. The single fare is £3. Service runs from 6:40 AM to 11 PM, at intervals of about 20 minutes (after 8 PM buses run every hour), to as far as Busaras, Dublin's main bus station, behind the Custom House on the northside. Journey time from the airport to the city center is normally 30 minutes, but it may be longer in heavy traffic.

A taxi is a quicker alternative than the bus to get from the airport to Dublin center. A line of taxis waits by the arrivals gateway; the fare for the 30-minute journey to any of the main city-center hotels is about £14 plus tip (tips don't have to be large but they are increasingly expected). It's advisable to ask about the fare before leaving the airport.

➤ SHUTTLE INFORMATION: **Dublin Bus** (tel. 01/873–4222). **Busaras** (tel. 01/830–2222).

Bus Travel Around Dublin

Dublin has an extensive network of buses—most of them are green double-deckers. Timetables (£1.50) are available from Dublin Bus, staffed weekdays 9–5:30, Saturday 9–1. Fares begin at 55p and are paid to the driver, who will accept inexact fares, but you'll have to go to the central office in Dublin to pick up your change as marked on your ticket. Change transactions and the city's heavy traffic can slow service down considerably. Some bus services run on cross-city routes, including the smaller "Imp" buses, but most buses start in the city center. Buses to the north of the city begin in the Lower Abbey Street/Parnell Street area, while those to the west begin in Middle Abbey Street and in the Aston Quay area. Routes to the southern suburbs begin at Eden Quay and in the College Street area. A number of services are links to DART stations, and another regular bus route connects the two main provincial railway stations, Connolly and Heuston. If the destination board indicates AN LÁR, that means that the bus is going to the city center. Late-night buses run weekends, on the hour from midnight to 3 PM; the fare is £3.

➤ Bus Information: **Dublin Bus** (59 Upper O'Connell St., tel. 01/873–4222).

Bus Travel to and From Dublin

FROM THE U.K.

Numerous bus services run between Britain and Dublin, but **be ready for long hours on the road and possible delays.**

FARES & SCHEDULES

Pick up a timetable at any bus station or call the numbers below for a schedule. It's best to avoid Friday-evening and Sunday-morning travel, as this is when throngs of workers from the country return to and depart from Dublin on the weekends.

➤ Bus Information: **Bus Éireann** (tel. 01/836–6111). **National Express** (tel. 020/7724–0741). **Slattery's** (tel. 020/7482–1604). **Ulsterbus** (tel. 028/9033–3000).

Car Rental

If you are renting a car in the Irish Republic and intend to visit Northern Ireland (or vice versa), make this clear when you get your car, and check that the rental insurance applies when you cross the border.

Renting a car in Ireland is far more expensive than organizing a rental before you leave the United States. Rates in Dublin for an economy car with a manual transmission and unlimited mileage begin at US$40 a day/US$200 a week (January–April and November–December 15); US$45 a day/US$250 a week (May–June and September–October); and US$60 a day/US$320 a week (July–August and December 16–31). This includes the Republic's 12½% tax on car rentals.

➤ Major Agencies: **Alamo** (tel. 800/522–9696; 020/8759–6200 in the U.K.). **Avis** (tel. 800/331–1084; 800/331–1084 in Canada; 02/9353–9000 in Australia; 09/525–1982 in New Zealand). **Budget** (tel. 800/527–0700;0870/607–5000 in the U.K., through affiliate

Europcar). **Dollar** (tel. 800/800–6000; 0124/622–0111 in the
U.K.,through affiliate Sixt Kenning; 02/9223–1444 in Australia).
Hertz (tel. 800/654–3001; 800/263–0600 in Canada;020/8897–
2072 in the U.K.; 02/9669–2444 in Australia; 09/256–8690 in
New Zealand). **National Car Rental** (tel. 800/227–7368; 020/
8680–4800 in the U.K., where it is known as National Europe).

➤ In Dublin: **Avis** (1 Hanover St. E, tel. 01/677–5204; Dublin
Airport, tel. 01/844–5204); **Budget** (151 Lower Drumcondra Rd.,
tel. 01/837–9802; Dublin Airport, tel. 01/844–5919); **Dan Dooley**
(42–43 Westland Row, tel. 01/677–2723; Dublin Airport, tel. 01/
844–5156); **Hertz** (Leeson St. Bridge, tel. 01/660–2255; Dublin
Airport, tel. 01/844–5466); **Murray's Rent-a-Car** (Baggot St.
Bridge, tel. 01/668–1777; Dublin Airport, tel. 01/844–4179).

INSURANCE
When driving a rented car you are generally responsible for any
damage to or loss of the vehicle. Before you rent see what coverage
your personal auto-insurance policy and credit cards already
provide. Collision policies that car-rental companies sell for
European rentals usually do not include stolen-vehicle coverage.
Before you buy it, check your existing policies—you may already
be covered.

REQUIREMENTS & RESTRICTIONS
In Dublin your own driver's license is acceptable. An International
Driver's Permit is a good idea; it's available from the American
or Canadian automobile association, and, in the United Kingdom,
from the Automobile Association or Royal Automobile Club. These
international permits are universally recognized, and having one
in your wallet may save you a problem with the local authorities.

Most rental companies require you to be over 23 to rent a car
in Ireland (a few will rent to those over 21) and to have had a
license for over a year. Some companies also refuse to rent to
visitors over 70.

Car Travel

The number of cars in Ireland has grown exponentially in the last few years, and nowhere has their impact been felt more than in Dublin, where the city's complicated one-way streets are congested during the morning and evening rush hours and often during much of the rest of the day. If you can, avoid driving a car except to get you into and out of the city, and be sure to ask your hotel or guest house for clear directions to get you out of the city.

RULES OF THE ROAD

The Irish, like the British, **drive on the left-hand side of the road.** Safety belts must be worn by the driver and front passenger, and children under 12 must travel in the back. It is compulsory for motorcyclists and their passengers to wear helmets.

Drunk-driving laws are strict. Ireland has a Breathalyzer test, which the police can administer anytime. If you refuse to take it, the odds are you'll be prosecuted anyway. As always, the best advice is **don't drink if you plan to drive.**

Consumer Protection

Whenever shopping or buying travel services in Dublin, **pay with a major credit card** so you can cancel payment or get reimbursed if there's a problem. If you're doing business with a particular company for the first time, **contact your local Better Business Bureau and the attorney general's offices** in your own state and the company's home state, as well. Have any complaints been filed? Finally, if you're buying a package or tour, always **consider travel insurance** that includes default coverage (☞ Insurance, *below*).

➤ **BBBs: Council of Better Business Bureaus** (4200 Wilson Blvd., Suite 800, Arlington, VA 22203, tel. 703/276–0100, fax 703/525–8277 www.bbb.org).

Customs & Duties

When shopping, **keep receipts** for all purchases. Upon reentering the country, **be ready to show customs officials what you've bought.** If you feel a duty is incorrect or object to the way your clearance was handled, note the inspector's badge number and ask to see a supervisor. If the problem isn't resolved, write to the appropriate authorities, beginning with the port director at your point of entry.

IN IRELAND

Duty-free allowances have been abolished for those traveling between countries in the European Union (Austria, Belgium, Denmark, Finland, France, Germany, Greece, Ireland, Italy, Luxembourg, the Netherlands, Portugal, Spain, Sweden, the United Kingdom, but not the Channel Islands).

For goods purchased outside the EU, you may import duty-free: (1) 200 cigarettes or 100 cigarillos or 50 cigars or 250 grams of smoking tobacco; (2) 2 liters of wine, and either 1 liter of alcoholic drink over 22% volume or 2 liters of alcoholic drink under 22% volume (sparkling or fortified wine included); (3) 50 grams of perfume and ¼ liter of toilet water; and (4) other goods to a value of £142 per person (£73 per person for travelers under 15 years of age).

Goods that cannot be freely imported to the Irish Republic include firearms, ammunition, explosives, illegal drugs, indecent or obscene books and pictures, oral smokeless tobacco products, meat and meat products, poultry and poultry products, plants and plant products (including shrubs, vegetables, fruit, bulbs, and seeds), domestic cats and dogs from outside the United Kingdom, and live animals from outside Northern Ireland.

➤ INFORMATION: **Customs and Excise** (Irish Life Building, 2nd floor, Middle Abbey St., Dublin 1, tel. 01/878–8811).

IN AUSTRALIA

Australian residents who are 18 or older may bring home A$400 worth of souvenirs and gifts (including jewelry), 250 cigarettes or 250 grams of tobacco, and 1,125 ml of alcohol (including wine, beer, and spirits). Residents under 18 may bring back A$200 worth of goods. Prohibited items include meat products. Seeds, plants, and fruits need to be declared upon arrival.

➤ INFORMATION: **Australian Customs Service** (Regional Director, Box 8, Sydney, NSW 2001, tel. 02/9213–2000, fax 02/9213–4000).

IN CANADA

Canadian residents who have been out of Canada for at least 7 days may bring home C$500 worth of goods duty-free. If you've been away less than 7 days but more than 48 hours, the duty-free allowance drops to C$200; if your trip lasts 24–48 hours, the allowance is C$50. You may not pool allowances with family members. Goods claimed under the C$500 exemption may follow you by mail; those claimed under the lesser exemptions must accompany you. Alcohol and tobacco products may be included in the 7-day and 48-hour exemptions but not in the 24-hour exemption. If you meet the age requirements of the province or territory through which you reenter Canada, you may bring in, duty-free, 1.14 liters (40 imperial ounces) of wine or liquor or 24 12-ounce cans or bottles of beer or ale. If you are 16 or older you may bring in, duty-free, 200 cigarettes and 50 cigars. Check ahead of time with Revenue Canada or the Department of Agriculture for policies regarding meat products, seeds, plants, and fruits.

You may send an unlimited number of gifts worth up to C$60 each duty-free to Canada. Label the package UNSOLICITED GIFT—VALUE UNDER $60. Alcohol and tobacco are excluded.

➤ INFORMATION: **Revenue Canada** (2265 St. Laurent Blvd. S, Ottawa, Ontario K1G 4K3, tel. 613/993–0534, 800/461–9999 in Canada, fax 613/957–8911, www.ccra-adrc.gc.ca).

IN NEW ZEALAND

Homeward-bound residents 17 or older may bring back NZ$700 worth of souvenirs and gifts. Your duty-free allowance also includes 4.5 liters of wine or beer; one 1,125-ml bottle of spirits; and either 200 cigarettes, 250 grams of tobacco, 50 cigars, or a combination of the three up to 250 grams. Prohibited items include meat products, seeds, plants, and fruits.

➤ INFORMATION: **New Zealand Customs** (Custom House, 50 Anzac Ave., Box 29, Auckland, New Zealand, tel. 09/359–6655, fax 09/359–6732).

IN THE U.K.

If you are a U.K. resident and your journey was wholly within the European Union (EU), you won't have to pass through customs when you return to the United Kingdom. If you plan to bring back large quantities of alcohol or tobacco, check EU limits beforehand.

➤ INFORMATION: **HM Customs and Excise** (Dorset House, Stamford St., Bromley, Kent BR1 1XX, tel. 020/7202–4227).

IN THE U.S.

U.S. residents who have been out of the country for at least 48 hours (and who have not used the US$400 allowance or any part of it in the past 30 days) may bring home US$400 worth of foreign goods duty-free. U.S. residents 21 and older may bring back 1 liter of alcohol duty-free. In addition, regardless of your age, you are allowed 200 cigarettes and 100 non-Cuban cigars. Antiques, which the U.S. Customs Service defines as objects more than 100 years old, enter duty-free, as do original works of art done entirely by hand, including paintings, drawings, and sculptures.

You may also send packages home duty-free: up to US$200 worth of goods for personal use, with a limit of one parcel per addressee per day (except alcohol or tobacco products or perfume worth more than US$5); label the package PERSONAL USE and attach a list of its contents and their retail value. Do not label the package UNSOLICITED GIFT or your duty-free exemption will drop to US$100. Mailed items do not affect your duty-free allowance on your return.

➤ INFORMATION: **U.S. Customs Service** (1300 Pennsylvania Ave. NW, Washington, DC 20229, www.customs.gov; inquiries tel. 202/354–1000; complaints c/o Office of Regulations and Rulings; registration of equipment c/o Resource Management, tel. 202/927–0540).

Dining

In the quite recent past people seldom came to Ireland to eat. In fact, tourists often shared jokes about the stodgy, overcooked, slightly gray food they were often served up. But the last decade has seen rapid change in all aspects of Irish life, and that includes food and drink. The country is going through a culinary renaissance, and Dublin chefs are leading the charge. They are putting nouvelle spins on traditional Irish favorites. And, spurred on by a wave of new immigration, ethnic eateries of all types have sprung up in most major towns and cities.

The restaurants we list are the cream of the crop in each price category. For information about restaurants beyond those reviewed in our guide, look for dining guides available from the Irish Tourist Board (ITB) (☞ Visitor Information, *below*).

Embassies

➤ **AUSTRALIA:** (Fitzwilton House, Fitzwilton Terr., Dublin 2, tel. 01/676–1517).

➤ **CANADA:** (65 St. Stephen's Green, Dublin 2, tel. 01/478–1988).

➤ **UNITED KINGDOM:** (29 Merrion Rd., Dublin 2, tel. 01/205–3700).

➤ **UNITED STATES:** (42 Elgin Rd., Ballsbridge, Dublin 4, tel. 01/668–8777).

Emergencies

➤ DOCTORS AND DENTISTS: **Eastern Help Board** (tel. 01/679–0700). **Dublin Dental Hospital** (20 Lincoln Pl., tel. 01/662–0766).

➤ EMERGENCY SERVICES: **Gardai (police), ambulance, or fire** (tel. 999).

➤ HOSPITALS: **Beaumont** (Beaumont Rd., tel. 01/837–7755). **Mater** (Eccles St., tel. 01/830–1122). **St. James's** (1 James St., tel. 01/453–7941). **St. Vincent's** (Elm Park, tel. 01/269–4533).

➤ PHARMACIES: **Hamilton Long** (5 Upper O'Connell St., tel. 01/874–8456) **Temple Bar Pharmacy** (20 E. Essex St., Temple Bar, tel. 01/670–9751).

Holidays

Irish national holidays are as follows: January 1 (New Year's); March 17 (St. Patrick's Day); April 13, 2001 (Good Friday); April 16, 2001 (Easter Monday); May 1 (May Day); June 4 and August 6, 2001 (summer bank holidays); October 29, 2001 (autumn bank holiday); and December 25–26 (Christmas and St. Stephen's Day). If you plan to visit at Easter, remember that theaters and cinemas are closed for the last three days of the preceding week.

Insurance

The most useful travel insurance plan is a comprehensive policy that includes coverage for trip cancellation and interruption, default, trip delay, and medical expenses (with a waiver for preexisting conditions).

Without insurance you will lose all or most of your money if you cancel your trip, regardless of the reason. Default insurance covers you if your tour operator, airline, or cruise line goes out of business. Trip-delay covers expenses that arise because of bad weather or mechanical delays. Study the fine print when comparing policies.

Always **buy travel policies directly from the insurance company**; if you buy them from a cruise line, airline, or tour operator that goes out of business you probably will not be covered for the agency or operator's default, a major risk. Before making any purchase, **review your existing health and home-owner's policies** to find what they cover away from home.

➤ TRAVEL INSURERS: In the United States: **Access America** (6600 W. Broad St., Richmond, VA 23230, tel. 804/285–3300 or 800/284–8300, fax 804/673–1583, www.previewtravel.com), **Travel Guard International** (1145 Clark St., Stevens Point, WI 54481, tel. 715/345–0505 or 800/826–1300, fax 800/955–8785, www.noelgroup.com). In Canada: **Voyager Insurance** (44 Peel Center Dr., Brampton, Ontario L6T 4M8, tel. 905/791–8700, 800/668–4342 in Canada).

➤ INSURANCE INFORMATION: In the United Kingdom: **Association of British Insurers** (51–55 Gresham St., London EC2V 7HQ, tel. 020/7600–3333, fax 020/7696–8999, www.abi.org.uk). In Australia: **Insurance Council of Australia** (tel. 03/9614–1077, fax 03/9614–7924).

Lodging

The Irish Tourist Board (ITB) has an official grading system and publishes a list of "approved accommodations," which includes hotels, guest houses, bed-and-breakfasts, farmhouses, hostels, and camping parks. For each accommodation, the list gives a maximum charge that no hotel may exceed without special authorization. Prices must be displayed in every room, so if the hotel oversteps its limit, do not hesitate to complain to the hotel manager and/or the ITB. The ITB also distributes five accommodation guides, covering various kinds of lodgings, which are free if obtained in the United States (☞ Visitor Information, *below*).

The lodgings we list are the cream of the crop in each price category. We always list the facilities that are available—but we don't specify whether they cost extra: when pricing accommodations, always ask what's included and what costs extra. Especially in inexpensive places, some baths may contain a tub and shower, while others may have a shower only. Breakfast will likely be included in the price of your accommodation, except at large hotels. **Inquire when booking about bathing facilities and meals if you have specific concerns or needs.**

Money Matters

A modest hotel in Dublin costs about £100 a night for two; this figure can be reduced to under £70 by staying in a registered guest house or inn, and reduced to less than £35 by staying in a suburban B&B. Lunch, consisting of a good one-dish plate of bar food at a pub, costs around £6; a sandwich at the same pub, about £2. In Dublin's better restaurants, dinner will run around £20–£30 per person, excluding drinks and tip. Theater and entertainment in most places are inexpensive—about £14 for a good seat, and double that for a big-name, pop-music concert. For the price of a few drinks and a small entrance fee of about £1.50, you can spend a memorable evening at a *seisun* (pronounced *say-shoon*) in a music pub. Entrance to most public galleries is free, but stately homes and similar attractions normally charge about £3 per person. In Dublin, a cup of coffee costs 90p; a pint of beer, £2.50; a soda, £1; and a 2-km (1-mi) taxi ride, £4.50.

ATMS
Most major banks are connected to CIRRUS or PLUS systems; there is a four-digit maximum for PIN numbers.

CREDIT CARDS
Throughout this guide, the following abbreviations are used: **AE,** American Express; **DC,** Diner's Club; **MC,** MasterCard; and **V,** Visa. The Discover Card is not honored in Ireland.

➤ REPORTING LOST CARDS: **American Express** (tel. 0353/1205–5111).
Diners Club (tel. 0353/661–1800). **MasterCard** (tel. 0353/679–
8436). **Visa** (tel. 0353/668–5500).

CURRENCY

The unit of currency in the Irish Republic is the pound or punt,
pronounced *poont*. It is divided into 100 pence (abbreviated 100p).
In this guide, the £ sign refers to the Irish pound; the British
pound is referred to as the pound sterling and is written UK£.

Irish notes come in denominations of £100, £50, £20, £10, and
£5. Coins are available as £1, 50p, 20p, 10p, 5p, 2p, and 1p, and
they are not exchangeable outside the Republic of Ireland.

Ireland is a member of the European Monetary Fund (EMU) and
since January 1, 1999 all prices have been quoted in pounds and
euros. Noncash transactions, including credit-card payments,
can be quoted in euros. January 2002 will see the introduction of
the euro coins and notes, as well as the gradual withdrawal of the
local currency.

CURRENCY EXCHANGE

For the most favorable rates, **change money through banks.**
Although ATM transaction fees may be higher abroad than at
home, ATM rates are excellent because they are based on wholesale
rates offered only by major banks. You won't do as well at exchange
booths in airports or rail and bus stations, in hotels, in restaurants,
or in stores. To avoid lines at airport exchange booths, **get a bit
of local currency before you leave home.**

Dollars and British pounds are accepted only in large hotels and
shops geared to tourists. Elsewhere you will be expected to use
Irish currency.

At press time, the punt stood at around US$1.09, Canadian $1.68,
UK£.77, Australian $2.08, and New Zealand $2.70; however,
these rates will inevitably change both before and during 2001;
keep a sharp eye on the exchange rate.

➤ EXCHANGE SERVICES: **International Currency Express** (tel. 888/278–6628 for orders, www.foreignmoney.com). **Thomas Cook Currency Services** (tel. 800/287–7362 for telephone orders and retail locations, www.us.thomascook.com).

TRAVELER'S CHECKS

Traveler's checks are widely accepted in restaurants, hotels, shops, and stores throughout Ireland. However, if you're going to rural areas and small towns, go with cash; traveler's checks are best used in cities. Lost or stolen checks can usually be replaced within 24 hours. To ensure a speedy refund, buy your own traveler's checks—don't let someone else pay for them: irregularities like this can cause delays. The person who bought the checks should make the call to request a refund.

Packing

You can experience all four seasons in one day, so pack accordingly. Even in July and August, the hottest months of the year, a heavy sweater and a good waterproof coat or umbrella are essential. You should **bring at least two pairs of walking shoes**: it can and does rain at any time of the year, and shoes can get soaked in minutes.

The Irish are generally informal about clothes. In the more expensive hotels and restaurants most people dress formally for dinner, and a jacket and tie may be required in bars after 7 PM, but very few places operate a strict dress policy. Younger travelers should note that old or tattered blue jeans are forbidden in certain bars and dance clubs.

Passports & Visas

When traveling internationally, **carry your passport even if you don't need one** (it's always the best form of I.D.) and **make two photocopies of the data page** (one for someone at home and another for you, carried separately from your passport). If you lose your passport, promptly call the nearest embassy or consulate and the local police.

ENTERING IRELAND

All U.S., Canadian, Australian, and New Zealand citizens, even infants, need a valid passport to enter Ireland for stays of up to 90 days. Citizens of the United Kingdom, when traveling on flights departing from Great Britain, do not need a passport to enter Ireland. Passport requirements for Northern Ireland are the same as for the Republic.

PASSPORT OFFICES

The best time to apply for a passport or to renew is in fall and winter. Before any trip, check your passport's expiration date, and, if necessary, renew it as soon as possible.

➤ AUSTRALIAN CITIZENS: **Australian Passport Office** (tel. 131232, www.dfat.gov.au/passports).

➤ CANADIAN CITIZENS: **Passport Office** (tel. 819/994–3500 or 800/567–6868, www.dfait-maeci.gc.ca/passport).

➤ NEW ZEALAND CITIZENS: **New Zealand Passport Office** (tel. 04/494–0700, www.passports.govt.nz).

➤ U.K. CITIZENS: **London Passport Office** (tel. 0870/521–0410) for fees and documentation requirements and to request an emergency passport.

➤ U.S. CITIZENS: **National Passport Information Center** (tel. 900/225–5674; calls are 35¢ per minute for automated service, $1.05 per minute for operator service).

Safety

The theft of car radios, mobile phones, cameras, video recorders, and other items of value from cars is common in Dublin and other major cities and towns. Never leave any valuable items on car seats or in the foot space between the back and front seats or in the glove compartments. In fact, never leave anything whatsoever in sight in your car—even if you're leaving it for only a short time. You should also think twice about leaving valuables in your car while visiting tourist attractions anywhere in the country.

Senior-Citizen Travel

To qualify for age-related discounts, **mention your senior-citizen status up front** when booking hotel reservations (not when checking out) and before you're seated in restaurants (not when paying the bill). When renting a car, ask about promotional car-rental discounts, which can be cheaper than senior-citizen rates.

➤ EDUCATIONAL PROGRAMS: **Elderhostel** (75 Federal St., 3rd floor, Boston, MA 02110, tel. 877/426–8056, fax 877/426–2166, www.elderhostel.org). **Interhostel** (University of New Hampshire, 6 Garrison Ave., Durham, NH 03824, tel. 603/862–1147 or 800/733–9753, fax 603/862–1113, www.learn.unh.edu).

Taxes

VALUE-ADDED TAX

When leaving the Irish Republic, U.S. and Canadian visitors **get a refund** of the value-added tax (VAT), which currently accounts for a hefty 21% of the purchase price of many goods and 12.5% of those that fall outside the luxury category. Apart from clothing, most items of interest to visitors, right down to ordinary toilet soap, are rated at 21%. Most crafts outlets and department stores operate a system called Cashback, which enables U.S. and Canadian visitors to collect VAT rebates in the currency of their choice at Dublin or Shannon Airport on departure. Otherwise, refunds can be claimed from individual stores after returning home. Forms for the refunds must be picked up at the time of purchase, and the form must be stamped by customs before leaving Ireland (including Northern Ireland). Most major stores deduct VAT at the time of sale if goods are to be shipped overseas; however, there is a shipping charge. VAT is not refundable on accommodation, car rental, meals, or any other form of personal services received on vacation.

When leaving Northern Ireland, U.S. and Canadian visitors can also get a refund of the 17.5% VAT by the over-the-counter and the direct-export methods. Most larger stores provide these services upon request and will handle the paperwork. For the over-the-counter method, you must spend more than £75 in one store. Ask the store for Form VAT 407 (you must have identification—passports are best), to be given to customs when you leave the country. The refund will be forwarded to you in about eight weeks (minus a small service charge) either in the form of a sterling check or as a credit to your charge card. The direct-export method, where the goods are shipped directly to your home, is more cumbersome. VAT Form 704/1/93 must be certified by customs, police, or a notary public when you get home and then sent back to the store, which will refund your money.

Global Refund is a V.A.T. refund service that makes getting your money back hassle-free. The service is available Europe-wide at 130,000 affiliated stores. In participating stores, **ask for the Global Refund form** (called a Shopping Cheque). Have it stamped like any customs form by customs officials when you leave the European Union. Then take the form to one of the more than 700 Global Refund counters—conveniently located at every major airport and border crossing—and your money will be refunded on the spot in the form of cash, check, or a refund to your credit-card account (minus a small percentage for processing).

➤ **V.A.T. REFUNDS: Global Refund** (707 Summer St., Stamford, CT 06901, tel. 800/566–9828, fax 203/674–8709, www. globalrefund.com).

By Taxi

Official licensed taxis, metered and designated by roof signs, do not cruise. Taxi stands are located beside the central bus station, at train stations, O'Connell Bridge, St. Stephen's Green, College Green, and near major hotels; the Dublin telephone directory has a complete list. The initial charge is £1.80 with an additional charge of about £1.60 a kilometer thereafter. The fare is displayed on a meter (make sure it's on). Alternatively, you may phone a taxi company and ask for a cab to meet you at your hotel, but this may cost up to £2 extra. Hackney cabs, which also operate in the city, have neither roof signs nor meters and will sometimes respond to hotels' requests for a cab. Negotiate the fare before your journey begins. Although the taxi fleet in Dublin is large, the cabs are nonstandard and some cars are neither spacious nor in pristine condition.

➤ Taxi Companies: **Cab Charge** (tel. 01/677–2222), **Metro** (tel. 01/668–3333), and **VIP Taxis** (tel. 01/478–3333).

Telephones

Ireland's telephone system is up to the standards of the United Kingdom and the United States. Direct-dialing is common; local phone numbers have five to eight digits. You can make international calls from most phones, and some cell phones also work here, depending on the carrier.

Do not make calls from your hotel room unless it's absolutely necessary. Practically all hotels add 200% to 300% to the cost of a call.

AREA & COUNTRY CODES

The country code for Ireland is 353, and the area code for Dublin is 01. When dialing an Irish number from abroad, drop the initial 0 from the local area code. The country code is 1 for the United States and Canada, 61 for Australia, 64 for New Zealand, and 44 for the United Kingdom.

DIRECTORY & OPERATOR ASSISTANCE

If the operator has to connect your call, it will cost at least one-third more than direct dial.

INTERNATIONAL CALLS

International dialing codes can be found in all telephone

directories. The international prefix from Ireland is oo. For calls to Great Britain, dial 0044 before the exchange code, and drop the initial zero of the local code. For the United States and Canada dial 001, for Australia 0061, and for New Zealand 0064.

LOCAL CALLS
To make a local call just dial the number direct.

LONG-DISTANCE CALLS
To make a long-distance call, just dial the area code, then the number. If you are dialing Northern Ireland from the Republic, dial 048 or 4428, followed by the new eight-digit number (e.g., For Belfast, dial either 048/90XX–XXXX or 4428/90XX–XXXX).

LONG-DISTANCE SERVICES
AT&T, MCI, and Sprint access codes make calling long distance relatively convenient, but you may find the local access number blocked in many hotel rooms. First ask the hotel operator to connect you. If the hotel operator balks, ask for an international operator, or dial the international operator yourself. One way to improve your odds of getting connected to your long-distance carrier is to travel with more than one company's calling card (a hotel may block Sprint, for example, but not MCI). If all else fails, call from a pay phone.

➤ ACCESS CODES: **AT&T Direct** (tel. 1800/550000). **MCI WorldPhone** (tel. 1800/555–1001). **Sprint International Access** (tel. 1800/552001).

PHONE CARDS
"Callcards" are sold in all post offices and at most newsagents. These come in denominations of 10, 20, and 50 units, and range in price from £2 for 10 calls to £16 for 100 calls. Card phones are now more popular than coin phones.

PUBLIC PHONES
Public pay phones are in all towns and villages. They can be found in street booths and in restaurants, hotels, bars, and shops, some

of which display a sign saying YOU CAN PHONE FROM HERE. There are currently at least three different models of pay phones in operation; read the instructions or ask for assistance. A local call costs 20p for three minutes; long-distance calls within Ireland are around 80p for three minutes.

Time

Dublin is 5 hours ahead of New York, 8 hours ahead of Los Angeles and Vancouver, 14 hours behind Auckland, and 11 hours behind Sydney and Melbourne.

Tipping

In some hotels and restaurants a service charge of around 10%—rising to 15% in a few plush spots—is added to the bill. If in doubt, ask whether service is included. In places where it is included, tipping is not necessary unless you have received particularly good service. But if there is no service charge, add a minimum of 10% to the total.

Tip taxi drivers about 10% of the fare displayed by the meter. Hackney cabs, who make the trip for a prearranged sum, do not expect tips. There are few porters and plenty of baggage trolleys at airports, so tipping is usually not an issue; if you use a porter, 50p is the minimum. Tip hotel porters about 50p per large suitcase. Hairdressers normally expect about £1. You don't tip in pubs, but for waiter service in a bar, a hotel lounge, or a Dublin lounge bar, leave about 50p.

Train Travel

An electric railway system, the DART (Dublin Area Rapid Transit) connects Dublin with Howth to the north and Bray to the south on a fast, efficient line. There are 25 stations on the route, which is the best means of getting to seaside destinations such as Howth, Blackrock, Dun Laoghaire, Dalkey, Killiney, and Bray.

The service starts at 6:30 AM and runs until 11:30 PM; at peak periods, 8–9:30 AM and 5–7 PM, trains arrive every five minutes. At other times of the day, the intervals between trains are 15 to 25 minutes. Tickets can be bought at stations, but it's also possible to buy weekly rail tickets, as well as weekly or monthly "rail-and-bus" tickets, from the Irish Rail Travek Centre. Individual fares begin at 65p and range up to £1.30. There are heavy penalties for traveling the DART without a ticket. Train services run from Heuston Station to Kildare Town west of Dublin via Celbridge, Sallins, and Newbridge, and from Connolly Station to more distant locations like Malahide, Maynooth, Skerries, and Drogheda to the north of Dublin and Wicklow and Arklow to the south.

➤ TRAIN INFORMATION: **Connolly Station** (Amiens St.).**DART** (tel. 01/836–6222).**Heuston Station** (End of Victoria Quay). **Irish Rail Travel Centre** (35 Lower Abbey St., tel. 01/836–6222).

Visitor Information

For information on travel in the Irish Republic, contact the **Irish Tourist Board** (ITB), known as Bord Fáilte (pronounced Board Falcha); its Web site is: www.ireland.travel.ie.

➤ **ITB: Ireland** (Baggot St. Bridge, Dublin 2, tel. 01/602–4000, 669/792083, or 1850/230330 [within Ireland], fax 01/602–4100). **U.S.** (345 Park Ave., New York, NY 10154, tel. 212/418–0800 or 800/223–6470, fax 212/371–9052). **U.K.** (Ireland House, 150 New Bond St., London W1Y 0AQ, tel. 020/7493–3201, fax 020/7493–9065).

➤ IN DUBLIN: **Bord Fáilte** (Baggot St. Bridge, tel. 1850/230330 (within Ireland) or 01/602-4000, fax 01/602–4100). **Dublin Tourism** (Suffolk St., just off Grafton St., tel. 01/605–7700 or 1850/230330 within Ireland, fax 01/605–7787). **Temple Bar Information Centre** (18 Eustace St., tel. 01/671–5717, fax 01/677–2525).

Web Sites

Do check out the World Wide Web when you're planning. You'll find everything from up-to-date weather forecasts to virtual tours of famous cities.

For a comprehensive directory of sites on Ireland, visit **www. paddynet.com**. Some of the most popular sites (note that their log-on addresses are subject to change) are: Best of Ireland (www.iol.ie/~discover/welcome.htm); Every Celtic Thing on the Web (www.mi.net/users/ang/angris.html); and Heritage Ireland (www.heritageireland.ie). In addition, many of the leading newspapers of Ireland have their own Web sites, which can be gold mines of timely information about special events, the latest restaurants, and newest cultural happenings. Track down these newspaper Web sites using a search engine.

When to Go

Summer remains the most popular time to visit Ireland, and for good reason. The weather is pleasant, the days are long (daylight lasts until after 10 in late June and July), and the countryside is green and beautiful. But there will be crowds in popular holiday spots, and prices for accommodations are at their peak.

Fall and spring are good times to travel (late September can often be dry and warm, although the weather can be unpredictable). Seasonal hotels, restaurants, and accommodations usually close from early- or mid-November until mid-March or Easter. During this off-season, prices are considerably lower than in summer, but your selection of hotels and restaurants is limited, and many minor attractions also close. St. Patrick's Week in March gives a focal point to a spring visit, but some American visitors may find the saint's-day celebrations a little less enthusiastic than the ones back home. Dublin, however, welcomes American visitors on March 17 with a weekend-long series of activities, including a parade and the Lord Mayor's Ball. If you're planning an Easter

Your checklist for a perfect journey

WAY AHEAD

- Devise a trip budget.

- Write down the five things you want most from this trip. Keep this list handy before and during your trip.

- Make plane or train reservations. Book lodging and rental cars.

- Arrange for pet care.

- Check your passport. Apply for a new one if necessary.

- Photocopy important documents and store in a safe place.

A MONTH BEFORE

- Make restaurant reservations and buy theater and concert tickets. Visit fodors.com for links to local events.

- Familiarize yourself with the local language or lingo.

TWO WEEKS BEFORE

- Replenish your supply of medications.

- Create your itinerary.

- Enjoy a book or movie set in your destination to get you in the mood.

- Develop a packing list. Shop for missing essentials. Repair and launder or dry-clean your clothes.

A WEEK BEFORE

- Stop newspaper deliveries. Pay bills.

- Acquire traveler's checks.

- Stock up on film.

- Label your luggage.

- Finalize your packing list— take less than you think you need.

- Create a toiletries kit filled with travel-size essentials.

- Get lots of sleep. Don't get sick before your trip.

A DAY BEFORE

- Drink plenty of water.

- Check your travel documents.

- Get packing!

DURING YOUR TRIP

- Keep a journal/scrapbook.

- Spend time with locals.

- Take time to explore. Don't plan too much.

visit, don't forget that most theaters close from Thursday to Sunday of Holy Week (the week preceding Easter), and all bars and restaurants, except those serving hotel residents, close on Good Friday.

If you want to feel like the only tourist in town, **try a winter visit.** Many hotels arrange special Christmas packages with entertainment and outdoor activities; horse races and hunting trips abound. Mid-November to mid-February is either too cold or too wet for all but the keenest golfers, but some of the coastal links courses are playable in almost any weather. There are cheerful open fires in almost all hotels and bars, and, with extra time on their hands, people tend to take an added interest in visitors.

CLIMATE
What follows are average daily maximum and minimum temperatures for Dublin.

CLIMATE CHART

Jan.	47F	8C	May	59F	15C	Sept.	63F	17C
	34	1		43	6		49	9
Feb.	47F	8C	June	65F	18C	Oct.	58F	14C
	36	2		49	9		43	6
Mar.	50F	10C	July	68F	20C	Nov.	50F	10C
	38	3		52	11		40	4
Apr.	56F	13C	Aug.	67F	20C	Dec.	47F	8C
	40	4		52	11		38	3

➤ FORECASTS: **Weather Channel Connection** (tel. 900/932–8437), 95¢ per minute from a Touch-Tone phone.

INDEX

H

Halo, 83
Ha'penny Bridge, 34, 36
Ha'penny Bridge Galleries, 94
Harbour Master, 83–84
Harcourt Hotel, 117
Harolds Cross, 105
Health clubs, 103
Henry Street, 88
Heraldic Museum, 26
Herbert Park, 102, 104
Herbert Park Hotel, 138
Hermitage, 103
Hibernian Hotel, 139
HMV (music store), 97
Hodges Figgis (bookstore), 95
Hogan's (pub), 113
Holidays, 155
Homes, historic, 18–19, 26–27, 32, 53–54
Hop Store, 44
Horse racing, 105–106
Horseback riding, 103
Horseshoe Bar (pub), 19, 113
Hospitals, 155
Hotels, 19, 127–128, 156–157
City Center (Northside), 140–142
City Center (Southside), 128–133
Dublin Airport area, 143–144
South City Center—Ballsridge, 137–140
South County Dublin Suburbs, 142–143
Temple Bar, 136–137

House of Ireland (shop), 96
House of Lords, 13
Hugh Lane Municipal Gallery of Modern Art, 52, 56–57
Hughes & Hughes (bookstores), 95
Huguenot Cemetery, 12, 17

I

Il Primo, 75–76
Ilac Center (shopping center), 89
Insurance, travel, 149, 155–156
International Bar, 122
Irish Cabaret, 117
Irish Film Centre (IFC), 34, 36, 121
Irish Film Centre Café, 37
Irish Jewish Museum, 60, 61
Irish Museum of Modern Art, 47
Irish music and dancing, 117
Irish Rugby Football Union, 106
Irish Tourist Board, 166
Iveagh Fitness Club, 103
Iveagh Gardens, 18
Iveagh Market Hall, 49, 50

J

Jackie Fitness Centre, 103
James Joyce Cultural Centre, 52, 57
Jazz music, 121–122
Jervis Shopping Centre, 89
Jewelry stores, 95–96
JJ Smyth's (jazz club), 122
Joe Daly, 102
Jogging, 104
John Fallons (pub), 111